Moral and Political Philosophy

by
James H. Rutherford

TOP 20 PUBLISHING
COLUMBUS, OHIO 43215
www.top20publishing.com

Dedicated to my mother

Gladys Freeland Rutherford

Table of Contents

Preface

The three central essays in this collection present a general framework of analysis for moral and political philosophy and examples of the usefulness of this framework. The logical progression thus begins with the second of these essays *An Ecological Organic Paradigm: A Framework of Analysis for Moral and Political Philosophy*. This essay describes a four-part framework of analysis based on a multidimensional understanding of human nature and ecology, with ecology being understood as the interaction between an organism and its environment. The usefulness of this framework is illustrated by applying it first to political philosophy in *The Moral Foundations of United States Constitutional Democracy: a Historical and Analytic Inquiry into the Primary Moral Value of Equality*. The framework is also then used in the third central essay to analyze an applied moral philosophy in *What Medical Ethics Have to Offer the Larger Fields of Moral and Political Philosophy*. The essays, however, are presented in the order in which they were originally written and they can be read that way.

The essays are closely interrelated, but they were originally presented to quite different audiences. There is thus some significant overlap, repetition and even duplication of some of the central themes. These are being applied in different contexts, however, and this is helpful for the purpose of illustration.

I also think it is useful for authors of this type of work to give some indication of their personal background and the influences in their lives. The last essay is a tribute to my father and it may in part serve this purpose. The occasion for writing this tribute was a distinguished alumni award that he received from his high school in Westlake, Ohio. I feel fortunate to have written this essay before he died at the age of 92. The book is dedicated to my mother, Gladys Rutherford, who was my first and best teacher. The first essay is on George Orwell simply because I wish it to be so.

The introduction is an overview and the place to begin.

Introduction

(The Framework of Analysis and the Issues Addressed)

A major theme of these essays is that most of philosophy in the past 100 years has been like the blind men describing the elephant—each perspective gives a reasonable description of a particular part, but none gives a coherent view of the "elephant." These essays present a very useful way of describing the "elephant" and in doing so they bring some coherence to moral and political philosophy.

The essays present a *framework of analysis* for moral and political philosophy. This four-part framework is based on a multidimensional understanding of human nature. It uses the perspective of the mind or consciousness and ecology, which is the interaction between an organism and its environment. It thus begins with our levels of awareness and relates them to the evolution and development of our mental capacities. The levels of awareness relate to our individual basic primal needs and desires, society, the natural world in which we live and finally our place in that world or metaphysics. The mental capacities that correlate with these levels of awareness are described as appetite, social consciousness, rational thought, and finally an integrative capacity that some might describe as the psyche or the soul. The integrative capacity and metaphysics have to do with orientation, integration, narrative, and meaning and purpose.

This four-part framework, which encompasses the individual, social, natural, and metaphysical perspectives, will be shown to be very useful as a framework of analysis for moral and political philosophy. This pattern will be described as being apparent in the evolutionary development of the brain (MacLean and Eccles) and the similar progressive development of our mental capacities through experience in childhood (Piaget), and the similar development of our moral capacities (Kohlberg). The essays then relate, in turn, these concepts from the life sciences to a similar pattern in folk psychology, the philosophy of Aristotle, Stevenson's categories for analyzing any philosophy, the meta-ethical cate-

3

gories, the different historical origins and meanings of the concept of equality, the division of powers in United States constitutional democracy, a four-part model for the causes of pain, and the four principles of medical ethics along with other examples. Many of the fashionable positions in the current climate of opinion in both moral and political philosophy will be challenged. The observation is also made that biology will probably become the prevailing paradigm or model of this century. The framework being described provides a methodology that is inclusive enough to bring some "consilience" to the life sciences, the social sciences, and the humanities, as well as some coherence to the categories of moral and political philosophy.

The usefulness of the four-part general framework of analysis is illustrated by applying it to the primary moral assertion of equality in United States constitutional democracy and then to the primary moral assertion of a respect for human life in medical ethics. It is pointed out that equality, and not freedom, is the primary moral value of United States constitutional democracy and that to properly convey the substantive as well as the procedural aspects of this value of equality one has to refer to our government as at least a *constitutional* democracy. The multidimensional aspects of human nature are reflected in our system of government by the division and balance of powers and the separation of religion and opinion from the coercive powers of government. The essays then also use this four-part framework of analysis to describe how the four principles of medical ethics are related to the primary moral assertion of a respect for human life and a multidimensional understanding of human nature. The essays also describe how, from its beginnings with Hippocrates, medicine has incorporated both science and an ethic, nature and nurture, and fact and value. It has been both descriptive and prescriptive. Furthermore, an association is made between the primary moral assertion of equality in constitutional democracy and the primary moral assertion of a respect for human life in medical ethics. They both represent a respect for persons and an

4

affirmation of human dignity and worth. The essays also describe how medical ethics at least have the capacity to address the need for dialogue and the capacity for accommodation in a pluralistic global community. The essays thus also address some of the pressing issues of our day, including the need for a stable world order.

Perhaps the easiest place to begin to describe this four-part multidimensional framework of analysis, however, is with folk psychology. Folk psychology has been called the "basic descriptive and explanatory conceptual framework with which all of us currently comprehend the behavior and mental life of our fellow humans and ourselves (Churchland 1995, 18–19)." Folk psychology intuitively and through self-reflection understands there to be physical, social, rational and spiritual aspects of human nature. A good example of this four-part description would be to consider what you might decide to do on a weekend morning. One of the tests of a theory should be whether it correlates with our everyday experiences and the way we actually live our lives.

On a weekend morning you probably take care of your morning routine and then have breakfast. To satisfy other physical needs you may decide that you need extra sleep or that you need to exercise because you have been behind a desk all week. You may also feel that you need to spend social time with the family and go to your child's soccer game or a community event. On the other hand you may have work that needs to be done by Monday for your job, the roof may have a hole in it that needs to be fixed before the next rain, or the grass may need to be mowed. You also may feel that you just need some time for thoughtful reflection with reading, a hobby, or attending a religious service. This is all that is meant by saying that human nature is multidimensional. All of these activities are valid and authentic, and they satisfy our physical, social, rational and metaphysical or spiritual needs. Often because of the constraints of time and other factors we have to choose between them, and yet we try to maintain some coherence and integrity in our lives.

This multidimensional understanding of human nature is not a modern or postmodern idea. It is a pre-modern idea. Plato discussed the triune soul. Aristotle described man as an animal, a political animal (meant to live in a *polis* or community), a rational animal, and a contemplative animal that seeks *eudaimonia* (variously translated as well-being, happiness, proper functioning, or meaning and purpose). Greek civilization began with primarily concrete descriptive thought in the time of Homer, progressed to predominately social thought in Athens at the time of Pericles, further developed rational and naturalistic thinking under Pythagoras, Euclid, Thucydides, and Hippocrates, and finally emphasized abstract thought with the classical Greek philosophers. This multidimensional understanding of human nature was related to the different ways that we interact with the world in which we live. It was often referred to as the organic paradigm, particularly when it was applied to social structure. It was eventually discarded after the Middle Ages because it also had been used to justify religious and political hierarchies. Plato had used this model in his writings to justify the rule of a philosopher-king. In the Middle Ages this paradigm, among others, was used to justify political class divisions and the rule of the king and the Pope.

Perhaps the central insight of these essays is that modern medicine uses these same categories, but not necessarily in a hierarchical manner. There is thus a reason to reconsider these categories and this multidimensional understanding of human nature as a framework of analysis for moral and political philosophy. This proves to be very useful as a means of critique and deeper analysis of those philosophies and ideologies that have been based primarily on only one aspect of human nature or have perhaps left out or excluded an aspect of human nature. One often does not have to argue that a particular philosophical position is wrong, but simply that it holds only one part of the "elephant" and that is not inclusive enough. A multidimensional understanding of human nature in the context of ecology often does not lead to certainty, but, on the other hand, it does not consider everything to be subjec-

6

tive, relative, arbitrary, or based only on material utility. The essays thus address not only some of the tragic ideologies of modernism and anti-modernism, but also what at least some consider to be the postmodern dilemma.

These essays of necessity use some philosophical jargon, but they are only affirming what has just been discussed concerning folk psychology and the similar categories used by Aristotle, because the pattern described by this framework of analysis holds across a wide range of scientific and social disciplines concerning human nature. This pattern, which is based on ecology, provides an explanatory link between nature and nurture, and an explanatory link between our inherent capacities and the development of those capacities through experience.

One of the distinguishing features of the history of Chinese science was that it was based primarily on the recognition of pattern. One is always reluctant to use tables and outlines because they seldom do justice to the nuances, variances and exceptions of the subject. They can in this case, however, be useful to help recognize the pattern which I have been discussing as *a useful framework of analysis*. The appendix at the end of this introduction illustrates a four-part framework of analysis that is based on the multiple dimensions of human nature and it should be useful as a summary and outline, as well as an illustration of a common pattern that can be seen across the basic sciences and moral and political philosophy. Some further commentary may be helpful.

A multidimensional understanding of human nature is compatible with the evolutionary development of the brain, which Paul MacLean described as beginning with a "reptilian complex" (concerned with such basic instincts as individual survival, hunger, and sex), progressing to a limbic system which involves emotions and a social capacity other than hierarchy, and then adding a neocortex which gives the capacity for reason (Sagan 1977, 57–83). To this can be added, at least functionally, what Sir John Eccles describes as the neo-neocortex, which involves an enlargement of the prefrontal cortex that includes the language centers and a capacity for more abstract thought (1989). This type of evolutionary development of the brain seems to be recapitulated or repeated in the mental development of the child through experience as described by Jean Piaget. This development begins with concrete self-interested thought, and then progresses to social, logical, and finally abstract thought (Inhelder and Piaget 1958). Lawrence Kohlberg described our moral development as following in the same pattern as our mental development (1981). Erick Erickson used a similar pattern to describe the predominant stages of the life cycle (1985).

It is this multidimensional understanding of human nature that brings some coherence to moral and political philosophy and the several ethical categories. Leslie Stevenson, in *Seven Theories of Human Nature* (1987), suggested that the best way to understand any philosophy or philosopher is to understand the assumptions being made concerning the nature of man, the nature of society, and the nature of the universe. Ever since the Copernican revolution, however, the last question has been divided into the scientific nature of the universe, which asks the question "How?", and the metaphysical nature of the universe which concerns man's place in the universe and asks the question "Why?" This multidimensional understanding of human nature also gives some coherence to the ethical categories. Deontological ethics (deon meaning duty), which are often metaphysically based, ask what is obligatory, what is right, or what is my duty. This is usually a universal rule-based ethic. Normative ethics, which are often, but not necessarily, rationally based, consequential, and utilitarian, ask what is good. Communitarian ethics ask what is fitting. An ethic that begins with the concerns of the individual (an egotistical ethic) is now interpreted primarily in terms of human rights, basic needs, and what is humane.

The usefulness of this four part general framework of analysis, which is described as a modern ecological organic paradigm (model), is illustrated by applying it first in a political context to the primary moral assertion of equality and the

8

foundations of United States constitutional democracy. It is then used to analyze the moral assertion of a respect for life and the applied moral philosophy of medical ethics. In philosophical jargon, the framework of analysis would be a meta-ethical explanatory theory and the primary moral assertions of equality and a respect for human life would give the framework normative, substantive, and procedural content.

In *The Moral Foundations of United States Constitutional Democracy: an Analytical and Historical Inquiry into the Primary Moral Concept of Equality* this four-part framework of analysis is used to describe the several origins of the concept of equality in Western civilization. The concept of equality has its historical origins in different moral and legal systems each of which was focused on a different aspect of human nature and the world in which we live, and each of which, therefore, had a different primary source of moral authority. Canon Law is based on a religious or *metaphysical* source of authority and it contains universal ethical principles of equality based on a reverence for God and reciprocity towards one's fellow humanity. Roman Law, on the other hand, incorporated significant aspects of *natural law* based on a perceived natural moral order in the universe, which everyone could understand with right reason. It contains concepts of equality based on reason and reversibility. English Common Law has a *communitarian* origin which bases concepts of equality on one's rights and responsibilities in society. Finally, there is an *individual* origin of concepts of equality in social contract theory, which is the basis of constitutional law. Social contract theory begins with the individual equal and free in a state of nature and concerned with human rights and the right to resist tyranny. United States constitutional democracy incorporates each of these concepts of equality and different aspects of human nature with a division of government into legislative, judicial and executive branches and the separation of religion and the expression of opinion from the coercive powers of government.

The essays contend that equality was the primary moral concept on which American constitutional democracy was

9

founded. The Constitution incorporates substantive concepts of equality and the democratic principle incorporates a procedural concept of equality. One can thus not understand or convey the moral foundations of our government without describing it as at least a *constitutional* democracy.

In *What Medical Ethics Has to Offer the Larger Fields of Moral and Political Philosophy* this four-part framework of analysis is then also applied to the four principles of medical ethics. The four principles of beneficence, nonmaleficence, justice, and autonomy are described as being based on a moral assertion of a respect for human life, and the multiple dimensions of human life. Furthermore, an association is made between the primary moral assertion of equality in the political realm and the primary moral assertion of a respect for human life in the realm of medical ethics. They both represent a respect for persons and an affirmation of our common human dignity and worth. That is, the pattern which is illustrated provides an explanatory link between an applied moral theory, such as medical ethics, which is based on a respect for human life, and that portion of the western liberal political tradition, which is based on the concept of equality. Furthermore, the moral assertion of a respect for human life in medical ethics is based on both the biological sciences and historical cultural sources, on both nature and nurture. Medical ethics approaches what Edward O. Wilson has called "consilience" between the biological sciences and the humanities and "reflective equilibrium," which in these essays is described as a balance of consciousness.

Medical ethics can provide a well-balanced source of affirmation, accommodation, moderation, coherence, and synthesis in a pluralistic world. They are one source of an applied moral philosophy that can provide cross-cultural understanding and enable ethical dialogue. Medical ethics have a lot to offer the larger fields of moral and political philosophy at this particular time in history, in part, because they have the capacity to accommodate pluralism in a global community.

The moral assertions of a respect for human life and universal equality, *which are both an affirmation of human dignity and*

10

worth, may be necessary for our collective survival and well-being in a pluralistic global community in a nuclear age. From a perspective based on ecology and co-evolution, the essays describe this affirmation as having individual, social, natural and metaphysical origins. A respect for human life and the concept of equality are both a self-affirmation and an affirmation of our common humanity. These essays help to explain why such an affirmation would appropriately include our basic needs, our social capacity, our capacity for reason and our capacity for interpretation and integration, whether understood as our psyche or soul. *A naturalized epistemology would include each of these ways of knowing, including metaphysical considerations.*

The essays challenge some of the prevailing ideas of the past 100 years.

The essays propose a four-part *framework of analysis* based on the interactions of ecology and a multidimensional understanding of human nature and the world in which we live. This framework is not meant to be exclusive, but it is felt to be very useful, both as a tool of analysis and a way of bringing some coherence to moral and political philosophy. The essays, however, challenge some of the prevailing academic assumptions and perspectives. Some of these challenges to prevailing ideas have already been proposed in the natural sciences, evolutionary theory, and philosophy, but they have not yet penetrated into the general academic environment or they are so new that they have not been fully vetted. Other challenges to the current climate of opinion are based on a new appreciation of parts of Aristotle's philosophy or some of the ideas of the Founding Fathers of United States constitutional democracy. The categories which are being proposed *as a framework of analysis* are also compatible with folk psychology or the way we generally live our lives. Therefore, if such ideas eventually lead to a change in the climate of opinion and even a change in the prevailing paradigm, they will probably in retrospect be considered to have always been obvious or even trivial. At this time, however, they are not. At this time we live following a century which coined the word genocide and which will also be identified with individual alienation—a time in which philosophy has been defined as "a discipline in crisis" and, perhaps not coincidently, a time in which we are also still striving for a stable world order.

1. The nature versus nurture controversy

The nature/nurture debate about human nature is a both/and rather than an either/or issue. This perspective is implicit in the broad concept of ecology as the interaction between an organism and its environment. The current form of this age old debate goes back to Darwin and Marx. It was exacerbated by the tragedies that resulted from both the eugenics and Social Darwinism of German fascism under Hitler and the social engineering and totalitarianism of the Marxist communist state under Stalin and Mao. More recently, the nature/nurture debate became a heated topic with the publication of *Sociobiology* in 1975 by Edward O. Wilson and the opposition to this book from a Marxist perspective by Steven Jay Gould and Richard Letowin. This all originated within the life science departments at Harvard University and the resulting general debate has not been a collegial one. It has been a major source of divisions within the life science communities and between the two cultures of the sciences and the humanities. Times and perspectives change, however, although sometimes slowly.

Evolutionary concepts have recently included a greater consideration of cooperation, altruism, "inclusive fitness," group and multilevel selection, and cultural evolution or co-evolution. Game theory (such as the The Prisoners Dilemma), concepts from computers and artificial intelligence (such as hardware and software, networking, parallel processing, and feedback), chaos and complexity theories (with such concepts as "convergence" and "synergy,"), and our changing perceptions in theoretical physics and astronomy (which should

12

keep us very humble) have also been changing our perspectives. As a result of the genome project, the sometimes multiple expressions of a "gene" are now beginning to be better understood in relation to other portions of the DNA code, the time and location of expression, chemical gradients, and other complex interactions and feedback mechanisms related to experience. On the other hand, our perceptions and experiences are now being perceived as more deeply related to our psychological orientations, the hormones and neurotransmitters of our physiology, and many subconscious and preconscious processes. Our mind is not a blank slate or a *tabla rasa* as explained by Steven Pinker in his recent work *The Blank Slate: the Modern Denial of Human Nature* (2003). The accumulating evidence for the interrelated combined effects of both nature and nurture is also made by Matt Ridley in his recent work *Nature via Nurture: Genes, Experience, and What Makes Us Human* (2003).

An article by Claudia Wallis in *Time* (May 10, 2004 pp. 56–65) on "What Makes Teens Tick," describes some of the progressive development of the brain as currently understood by neuroscience. The article supports the interaction of nature and nurture. Humans actually achieve their maximum brain cell density in utero at about the sixth month of gestation, with a dramatic pruning of unnecessary brain cells in the final months before birth. By the time the child is six the brain is 90% to 95% of its adult size. The second wave of proliferation and pruning then occurs, which may affect some of the higher mental functions only in the late teens. Between the ages of 6 and 12 the neurons develop more branch-like dendrites and make dozens of connections. The brain then develops more white matter composed of myelin sheaths that encase the axons and make the nerve signals faster and more efficient. The pruning, branching associations, and sheaths to improve transmission appear to be guided by genetics, but influenced by a use-it-or-lose-it principle related to experience and environment. Practicing the piano quickly thickens neurons in the brain regions that control the fingers. Teenagers are subjected

13

to a flood of hormones that particularly effect the emotions at a time when the prefrontal cortex, the part of the brain responsible for much of our rational judgment, is still maturing. Dr. Jay Giedd, who has been studying teenagers with brain imaging at the National Institutes of Mental Health, estimated that the brain is truly mature at about 25, the age at which you can rent a car. He is quoted as saying that "Avis must have some sophisticated neuroscientists." Our developed brains have several billions of neurons and at least 10 trillion synapses formed among those neurons.

The collection of essays in this book contends that nature and nurture are interactive and interrelated in the human condition. They resonate, in part, because the development of our mental and moral capacities through experience recapitulate or follow a similar pattern as the progressive evolutionary development of the functional capacities of our brain. The essays also contend that evolutionary theory needs to expand to include concepts of cultural evolution and, on the other hand, the totally cultural and behavioral concepts, such as historicism, need to extend "history" back into evolutionary time. We can, to some degree, transcend our natural environment and yet there are also natural constraints on our individual and social will. **Both nature and nurture are important in moral theory for they place limitations on each other.**

2. The facts versus values controversy

The nature/nurture debate has its roots in a more fundamental issue about facts and values. David Hume, a skeptic and a philosopher of the Scottish Enlightenment, wrote in *A Treatise of Human Nature* (1739), "In every system of morality. . . . I am surpriz'd to find, that instead of the usual copulations of propositions, *is,* and *is not,* I meet with no proposition that is not connected with an *ought* or an *ought not.* This change is imperceptible; but is, however, of the last consequence. For as this *ought,* or *ought not* expresses some new affirmation, 'tis necessary that it shou'd be observ'd and explain'd and at the same time that a reason shou'd be given, for what seems alto-

14

gether inconceivable, how this new relation can be a deduction from others, which are entirely different from it. . . . this small attention wou'd subvert all the vulgar systems of morality, and let us see, that the distinction of vice and virtue is not founded merely on the relations of objects, nor is perceived by reason (469–70)." The doctrine that one cannot infer an 'ought" from an "is" became known as Hume's Law.

The distinction of facts and values was further promoted at the beginning of the twentieth century by the philosopher G. E. Moore, who described the attempt to justify such normative valuation terms as "good" with empirical facts or scientific findings as "the naturalistic fallacy." The doctrine that there is a dichotomy or no relation between facts and values became a mantra of academics, particularly those of a Marxist persuasion, for the rest of the century.

In the quotation above, Hume wrote that "this *ought* or *ought not* expresses some new affirmation." In the previous century, Rene Descartes, a French mathematician and philosopher, had found this affirmation in the famous phrase *"Cogito ergo sum"* or "I think; therefore I am." Beginning from a position of radical skepticism, Descartes could doubt everything except his own thought as an affirmation of his being. He used this as his first principle of philosophy and from this he developed a philosophical system of rationalism based on deductive thought and reasoning. Hume, on the other hand, was essentially a non-cognitivist and he based this affirmation and his moral theory on sentiments, passions, and perceptions of pain and pleasure rather than reason. He wrote that "Reason is, and ought only to be, the slave of the passions . . . (1739, 415)"

An important contemporary critic of David Hume was Thomas Reid (1710–1796) who wrote *An Inquiry into the Human Mind on the Principles of Common Sense* (1764). Reid emphasized the constitution of man as the foundation of our first principles. He offered a naturalistic "common sense" psychology in which the creatures of nature, including human beings, are fitted out by the "mint of nature" with what is needed for survival, social actions, and a valid knowledge of the external world. This could be theistic or non-theistic, but for Reid, a minister in the Church of Scotland, it was ultimately due to a providential God.

Reid challenged Hume's position that we only know the world through perception mediated by our sense organs, that the constant conjunction or association of two things alone is the grounding of our belief in causation, and that morality is based only on the sentiments, passions, and emotions, as well as pleasure and pain. Reid, in some ways anticipating non-Euclidean geometry, demonstrated that the image of a right triangle when projected on the spherical retina of the eye is itself curved, yet we do not see a curved triangle, but the triangle as it is actually configured. We see what is really there and not just its impression on our senses. We are agents with active powers to achieve success within the natural order of things and this also accounts for what we bring to our concepts of causation. Reid's doctrine of common sense, which in the context of the present essays would be something similar to "folk psychology," was an attempt to combine elements of the school of reason (cognitivism) and the school of sentiment (non-cognitivism) in the area of morals. Recently in "The Neural Correlates of Moral Sensitivity," in the *The Journal of Neuroscience* (April 1, 2002, pp. 2730–2736), Jorge Moll and his colleagues used functional magnetic resonance imaging to demonstrate that moral behaviors are driven by both the emotional and the rational parts of the brain.

A more recent critique is in *The Collapse of the Fact/Value Dichotomy* (2002), by Hilaray Putnam, a widely respected Emeritus Professor of Philosophy at Harvard. Professor Putnam grants that it is occasionally important and useful to distinguish between factual claims and value judgments, but that the distinction becomes harmful when identified with a dichotomy between objective facts and subjective values. He takes a pragmatist position that a knowledge of facts presupposes a knowledge of values. He describes evaluation and description as interwoven and interdependent and he argues from a philosophical perspective that there is an entanglement of facts and values.

The current essays recognize that the respect for human life in medical ethics and the concept of equality and our common humanity in the Western liberal political tradition are affirmations and moral assertions, and that they have individual, social, natural and metaphysical origins. In this context of understanding human nature as being multidimensional, the relationship between facts and values is restated as **our perception of the facts is not the sole determinant of our values.**

3. "Depth" and "breadth" in moral philosophy and other distinctions in moral language.

In his 1871 book *The Descent of Man* Charles Darwin wrote: "The following proposition seems to me in a high degree probable—namely, that any animal whatever, endowed with well marked social instincts, the parental and filial affections being here included, would inevitably acquire a moral sense or conscience, as soon as its intellectual powers had become as well, or nearly as well developed, as in man (1:71–72)." Darwin also proposed group selection noting that, "advancement in the standard of morality will certainly give an immense advantage to one tribe over another. There can be no doubt that a tribe including many members who, from possessing in a high degree the spirit of patriotism, fidelity, obedience, courage and sympathy, were always ready to aid one another, and to sacrifice themselves for the common good, would be victorious over most other tribes; and this would be natural selection (1:166)." Darwin also recognized the cognitive fluidity of our multidimensional minds. He wrote of the evolution of a moral sense which he described as "a highly complex sentiment, having its first origin in the social instinct, largely guided by the approbation of our fellow-men, ruled by reason, self-interest, and in later times by deep religious feelings, confirmed by instruction and habit, all combined, constitute our moral sense and conscience (1:165–166)." Recently, brain scans have been used to show that people derive satisfaction from punishing norm violations even at a cost to themselves, as evidenced

17

by the activation of reward related brain circuits (Quervain, Dominique J.-F. de, et al., "Neurology of Altruistic Punishment" in *Science*, Aug. 27, 2004, pp. 1254–1258).

A few observations and distinctions are important, however, concerning moral theory and dialogue.

First, **it is important to recognize both** *"depth"* **and** *"breadth"* **in moral considerations.** Much of our discourse could be clarified by recognizing both "depth" and "breadth" in moral philosophy. There are, for example, two great moral traditions in Western civilization. The first is from classical civilization and is based primarily on a distinction of values regarding such things as truth, goodness and beauty and such qualities as virtue. The second concerns the equal dignity and worth of individuals as persons and is derived primarily from Judeo-Christian sources, such as the Golden Rule and *imago Dei* and later Kant's categorical imperative. The concept of moral "depth," refers to an affirmation of life and *a distinction of values that relates primarily to attributes and behavior.* The concepts of moral "breadth" extends this affirmation to the individual, the social community, our common humanity, concerns about the natural world in which we live, and metaphysical concepts of meaning and purpose. For a moral system to have sufficient "breadth," for example, there needs to be *a respect for persons* and *an affirmation of our common humanity.* The two ethical systems are often confused in dialogue when there is no recognition of the difference between an *equality of persons* and *a distinction of values that relates to attributes and behavior.* There also can be "moral" positions that are "narrow" and "shallow."

Second, relating to the previous discussion about nature and nurture, **morality entails both survival and well-being—both posterity and prosperity.** As a result of sexual reproduction, the human body is made up of both genetic cells and somatic cells. The genetic cells at least have the possibility of reproduction and continuity—the somatic cells in natural circumstances do not. What about us somatic cells? The somatic cells are concerned also about the quality of life.

18

Moral philosophy is thus concerned about both posterity and prosperity, about Darwinian survival and reproduction and also our individual and cultural well-being.

Third, **there is an expanding circle of our moral and political environment.** From the long-term perspective of anthropology, most of the societies in history have been kinship-dissent groups. Max Weber, an early twentieth century sociologist, coined the term "charismatic" to describe larger societies organized around a religious, political or military figure or movement. He also described a more recent and complex organization of society which he designated as legally based societies. We now, however, increasingly live in a pluralistic global community.

Fourth, **there is a distinction between negative and positive freedoms.** Negative freedoms are freedoms from the intervention of coercive power, such as most of those freedoms in the Bill of Rights. We seek freedom from the arbitrary will of others whether in the form of organized coercion or anarchy. Negative freedoms result primarily from voluntary or contractual inhibitions on our individual and social behavior. In peaceful times these do not usually cost us significant individual resources. They relate primarily to moral and political issues about what restraints we owe to each other as part of our common humanity. Positive freedoms are enabling freedoms, such as education, medical care, Social Security, and issues of the general welfare. They make claims upon other people. Positive freedoms are often achieved at the family and kinship level and they can also be based in voluntary associations, the trades and professions, social norms, religious institutions and philanthropies. Positive freedoms, however, often require a redistribution of resources that is accomplished with public programs, taxes and subsidies, and thus they are usually legislated or directed by a political process. We need both negative and positive freedoms for our survival and well-being.

Finally, if human nature is multidimensional, then there may sometimes be conflicting goals and desires, particularly in a pluralistic multicultural society. Therefore, **there** needs to be a generally accepted procedure for resolving disputed and conflicting values, issues and claims. In our legal system, for example, we use the procedure of a jury of fellow citizens to evaluate the evidence and facts in a case. At the top of our legal system we have a Supreme Court of nine justices to interpret the law and adjudicate conflicts in law and procedure.

4. A respect for human life is the unifying moral concept of the four principles of biomedical ethics.

Thomas Beauchamp and James Childress developed and taught the four principles of biomedical ethics of beneficence, nonmaleficence, justice and autonomy in their successive editions of the book *Principles of Biomedical Ethics*. They consider the four principles to be derived from the common morality (or all those who are serious about moral conduct and their moral responsibilities) and the historical moral traditions of medicine. They specifically state, however, that "in this 'theory,' there is no single unifying principle or concept—a traditional goal of ethical theory that seems now to be fading fast (2000, 405)." It should be noted, however, that neither Beauchamp nor Childress is a physician. More importantly, the moral assertion of a respect for human life can accommodate and be the basis for each of their described principles when human life and the world in which we live are understood to be multidimensional. Intuitionism is the view that there is a plurality of moral principles, each of which we can know directly. Beauchamp and Childress relied extensively on the intuitionist account of prima facie values by W.D. Ross in *The Right and the Good* (1930). Robert Audi is Professor of Philosophy and Professor of Business Ethics at the University of Notre Dame and Editor in Chief of *The Cambridge Dictionary of Philosophy*. In a recent work, *The Good and the Right: A Theory of Intuition and Intrinsic Value* (2004), Professor Audi also relies extensively on the work of W. D. Ross and concludes that, "In the practical domain, as in theoretical ethics, respect for persons is the fundamental attitude appropriate to the dignity of per-

20

sons, and the dignity of persons is the central higher-order pervasive value that encompasses the other values essential in grounding moral obligation (201)."

The essays in *Moral and Political Philosophy* consider a respect for human life to be the underlying moral assertion of the four principles of medical ethics. This moral assertion can be supported from the perspective of metaphysics, nature, society and the individual. In turn, a multidimensional understanding of human nature can be inclusive and supportive of our physical, social, mental, and psychic or spiritual needs. It is this multidimensional understanding of human nature and our interaction with the world in which we live that gives some coherence to the several ethical categories. The moral assertions of a respect for human life in medical ethics and equality in political philosophy are both an affirmation of our individual selves and the dignity and worth of our common humanity. It is in this context that medical ethics have the capacity to enable dialogue and accommodate pluralism in a global community. It is in this context that medical ethics have a lot to offer moral and political philosophy.

5. Our government is a constitutional democracy.

At the time of a clash of civilizations it is not unusual for both sides to re-examine, define, and even sometimes codify their basic values and cultural institutions in order to both preserve and convey their basic values and traditions. At the time of the fall of communism in the Soviet Union and in Eastern Europe, the United States did this poorly. It appears that we are making a similar mistake in our war against terrorism, which is very much a battle of ideas and ideologies and will have to be understood as such for any chance of a long-term resolution and reconciliation. **We are missing a defining opportunity in the history of the moral and political philosophy of the liberal tradition; first, by not defining our primary moral value as equality, understood as a respect for human life; and second, by not defining our government as a constitutional democracy, which is the only way to convey**

21

both the substantive and the procedural concepts of equality that it incorporates.

At the time of the fall of communism, however, the media, the academics, and our government almost universally described the United States as a *capitalistic* democracy. This was in part because we allowed the Soviet Union to describe their communism to be primarily an economic system rather than a totalitarian political system, which denied any concept of moral or political equality. The primary alternative to communism should have been *constitutional* democracy. The emphasis on capitalism, even for those countries without a legal or institutional substructure to support capitalism, was for the most part at least a short-term disaster. We can recognize today that we have paid a price in terms of our credibility in third world countries by defining ourselves at that time in a primary way as a capitalistic economic system rather than a constitutional democracy. Even in our own country, for example, the degree to which we are a social welfare state or a regulated capitalism is determined by a political process. Our political culture determines our economic policies. The same can ironically be said of the former Soviet Marxist state, which did not wither away, but collapsed of its own weight without the arbitrary use of coercive power to support it.

It is the constitutional aspects of our government, such as the Bill of Rights, that incorporate our substantive concepts of equality. The constitutional principles are placed beyond the majority rule of the legislative process. It is the democratic aspects of our government that incorporate the procedural aspects of equality, such as "one person, one vote."

6. The primary moral value of United States constitutional democracy is equality.

Jefferson, Madison, Tocqueville, and Lincoln all considered equality to be the primary moral principle of constitutional democracy. Yet again, in the current war on terrorism, which began on September 11, 2001, I cannot recall one

22

instance of even a mention of equality. The terrorist attack of 9/11 was an attack on our freedom and security and it is perhaps understandable that our values have subsequently been described primarily in those terms. The Declaration of Independence, however, was written in the manner of Euclidean geometry. Its first premise was that "all men are created equal" and that put everything that followed, including life, liberty and the pursuit of happiness, in a moral context. Even the great reformers, such as the women suffragettes and the Rev. Martin Luther King, Jr., did not repudiate these principles, but urged us to live up to them and place them into practice. A singular emphasis on freedom and liberty at this time may be good for rallying the nation, but it should also be understood that we are in a battle of ideas, in part, with a radical version of Islam. Islam, the religion of 1.2 billion people, is based on a submission to the will of God. Much of the liberty that we convey, on the other hand, is seen by others as the license and self-indulgence in our popular culture rather than the political concept of self-government. During the current war on terrorism it may be appropriate that we emphasize freedom, and to win this war we will need the cooperation of many countries that are not constitutional democracies. To win the peace, however, we will need to understand and convey that our primary moral value is universal equality. It is some recognition of our common humanity in a pluralistic world that makes the accommodation of a wide variety of attributes, cultural differences, desires, and beliefs possible without the use of coercion or being the cause of alienation.

Such concepts of equality are perhaps so ingrained in our own culture that we take them for granted and fail to reflect on them, to clarify and delineate their meaning, and to convey to others their significance. On the other hand, the enormous damages done recently in the court of world opinion concerning the issues of prisoner abuse in Iraq and our failure to voluntarily abide by the spirit of the Geneva Conventions would likely have been avoided if we had understood and attempted to convey our primary moral value as

23

equality, understood as an affirmation of the dignity and worth of our common humanity. The distortion of our moral compass has been from the top down, beginning with our academic elites.

7. Biology rather than physics will become the primary paradigm

Biology rather than physics will become the primary paradigm of this century. This is in part due to the genome project and the influence it will have on the direction of scientific research. It will also, however, be a result of a much broader understanding of co-evolution and our interaction with the world in which we live. It will be driven by very practical or pragmatic issues concerning life on earth and our need to live in what in many ways is becoming a global community. Biology will not become the new paradigm, however, until it develops a methodology and a multidimensional understanding of human nature that is broad enough to include not only the life sciences, but also the other basic sciences, the social sciences, and the humanities.

Epistemology is the study of ways of knowing and biology is an epistemic process (Rolston 1999, 70). Unlike physics and chemistry which relate to matter and energy, biology also relates to information, which is both genetic and cultural in human biology. In evolutionary biology and in culture the transmission of information is also historical. Life means the presence of intrinsic and functional values. Biological diversity and complexity are based on information about how to compose, maintain, reproduce and transmit life processes. This is the type of self-affirming information that is lost in the reduction of biology to physics and chemistry. In *Nature's Magic: Synergy in Evolution and the Fate of Humankind* (2003), Peter Corning has described the "synergy" to be found in living organisms, which explains in part their adaptive functions in a way that a reduction to physical and chemical elements does not. There are emergent properties, synergies, and functional and cultural values that exist and that are lost in the translation to the basic elements. By natural selection we are not indifferent to our fate and, to a degree, we are also capable of modifying our environment and transcending nature with our human individual and cultural values. It has been noted that life is a countercurrent to entropy and culture may be a countercurrent to natural selection.

In the opening paragraph of his book *Pragmatism: A New Name for Some Old Ways of Thinking* (1907), William James, quoted these words from Chesterton, "There are some people—and I am one of them—who think that the most practical and important thing about a man is still his view of the universe. We think that for a landlady considering a lodger, it is important to know his philosophy. We think that for a general about to fight an enemy, it is important to know the enemy's numbers, but still more important to know the enemy's philosophy. We think the question is not whether the theory of the cosmos effects matters, but whether, in the long run, any thing else effects them." James then stated, in this defining essay on pragmatism, that he thinks with Chesterton in this matter.

There are some very recent changes in perspective which place greater emphasis on ecology as the interaction between an organism and its environment. Holmes Rolston III (1999), has noted that adaptation, a central word in Darwinian theory, is an *ecological* word, not a *genetic* one. Elliot Sober and David Sloan Wilson, the authors of *Unto Others: the Evolution and Psychology of Unselfish Behavior* (1998), have been instrumental in the understanding of evolution as a multilevel process. Peter Corning, in his work, writes that evolution can even be understood as a collective survival enterprise. In Darwin's *Cathedral: Evolution, Religion, and the Nature of Society,* (2002) David Sloan Wilson also recognizes both factual and practical realism—a factual realism based on literal correspondence and a practical realism based on behavioral adaptedness. As an evolutionary biologist, Wilson also believes that adaptation and not rationality is the gold standard against which all other forms of thought must be judged and that a well adapted mind is ultimately an organ of survival. One could surmise also the entanglement of factual realism and practical realism and the importance of our metaphysical capacities for both our survival and our well-being. In moral terms these would include both a Socratic quest and a humanistic commitment, whether they are secular or religious. The Socratic quest, however, can result in an unproductive and pedantic skepticism without a humanistic commitment. A humanistic commitment, whether secular or religious, on the other hand, also needs to remain to some degree open-ended and questioning to avoid the excesses of what Eric Hoffer, after World War II and in a response to fanaticism of all kinds, described as the "true believer."

Why now?

In political philosophy, the international political tragedies of the twentieth century bear witness to the need for universal concepts of equality. It is difficult to imagine an adequate resolution of the global problems which have resulted from technology without a concept of universal equality and a respect for human life and our common humanity. Several writers have noted that our technical progress has far exceeded the parameters of our biological adaptive mechanisms and moral structures. In evolutionary theory this is sometimes referred to as the "nuclear trap." Recently, the two major political powers in the world had a nuclear defense policy of mutual assured destruction, with response time measured in minutes, which some believe could have been fatal for most of life on earth. Power politics as policy thus reaches an undesired absurdity in which it has the potential to be destructive not only of self, but also the foundations of much of life on earth. Among the problems which threaten the future of all peoples are those of nuclear or biological warfare, genetic engineering and population control in a time of scarce resources and a threatened environment, and the level of totalitarianism and terrorism which technology has made possible. Raoul Naroll, in *The Moral Order* (1983), called the creation of a stable human world order the deepest historical task of our times.

Discord and alienation often result when one of our levels of understanding is emphasized to the exclusion of the others, or when, as a society, we develop ideologies that relate to one of our concepts of metaphysics, nature, society, or the individual, but to the exclusion of the other three. In a pluralistic society there is a potential political problem when any one dimension of human nature is emphasized to the exclusion of the others or when any dimension of human nature is excluded or not taken into consideration.

Singular theories that have based order and moral authority on only material needs, an aspect of social conscience, reason, or a metaphysical/religious concept, or only on the individual, the state, natural science, or an ideology have often led to disintegration and individual and communal tragedy. By focusing on even perhaps a particular truth, in the quest for certainty, they have too easily justified the use of coercive force or been the cause of alienation. The quest for certainty understandably often seeks truth in only one parameter.

It is, important that we be able to understand and convey to the court of world opinion the moral concepts of a respect for human life and equality understood as a respect for persons and the inherent dignity and worth of our common humanity. This is important, for survival, well-being, the enjoyment of individual freedom and the progress of human liberty are not inevitable. They are contingent to a large degree, on our willingness and ability as moral agents to place our free will within ethical constraints. It is indeed the self-imposed ethical or moral foundations of government that change mere obedience to the coercive powers of government into a sense of consensual responsibility for a moral duty, a just order, the common good and human rights. The coercive powers of government are also needed less when those moral values and ethical constraints are incorporated into the culture and our intermediary social institutions, such as voluntary associations, education, law, medicine, economics, science, religion, and philosophy.

The Major Themes

The essays describe a very useful framework of analysis for moral and political philosophy based on ecology and a multidimensional understanding of human nature. This framework brings some coherence to the ethical categories.

The essays describe an explanatory link between nature and nurture, between our inherited capacities and the development of those capacities through experience. They thus provide a basis for "consilience" between the sciences and the humanities.

This framework of analysis and a multidimensional understanding of human nature do not necessarily lead to certainty, but this perspective also does not consider everything to be subjective, relative, arbitrary, or based only on material utility. The essays thus address not only some of the tragic ideologies of modernism and anti-modernism, but also what some have described as the postmodern condition.

The examples of the four principles of medical ethics and four historical concepts of equality in the Western liberal tradition and United States constitutional democracy are used to describe a "balance of consciousness." This "balance of consciousness" may eventually provide a new perspective on pragmatism. It may also lead to a "naturalized epistemology" that includes integrative/metaphysical perspectives and considerations of adaptive realism.

The essays suggest and predict that biology, rather than physics, will probably become the prevailing paradigm of this century. This will also probably not occur, however, until the life sciences develop a methodology and understanding of human nature that is broad enough to also be inclusive of the natural sciences, the social sciences, and the humanities.

A change in perspective requires a challenge to some of the ideas in the currently prevailing climate of opinion. There is an often useful distinction between nature and nurture and also between facts and values, but the essays challenge and reject an absolute separation of such categories and their characterization as dichotomies, for they are often entangled. The essays point out that moral decisions often include considerations of not only Darwinian survival, but also of well being. They point out that it is important in our dialogue to recognize both "depth" (a distinction of values that relates primarily to attributes and behavior) and "breadth" (which has to do primarily with inclusiveness). The essays note that ecology changes. It is thus also important in our dialogue to recognize the expanding circle of our moral and political environment, as well as a distinction between negative and positive freedoms. There also needs to be a generally accepted procedure for resolving disputed and sometimes conflicting values, issues and claims, a procedure where the means do justice to the ends.

Concerning political philosophy, the essays claim that we are missing a defining opportunity in the history of the Western liberal tradition by not defining our primary moral value as equality, understood as a respect for persons and the dignity and worth of our individual and common humanity, and by not defining, in discourse, our government as a constitutional democracy, which is the only way to understand and convey both the substantive and the procedural concepts of equality that it incorporates.

Concerning the applied moral philosophy of medical ethics, the essays assert that, from the perspective of the physician, a respect for human life is the underlying foundation of the four principles of beneficence, nonmaleficence, justice, and autonomy.

The essays describe the primary moral concept of equality in United States constitutional democracy and the moral assertion of a respect for human life in medical ethics to both be based on a multidimensional understanding of human nature, a respect for persons, and an affirmation of human dignity and worth. It is also noted that medical ethics are one source of an applied moral philosophy that can enable cross-cultural understanding and ethical dialogue. Medical ethics have a lot to offer moral and political philosophy at this particular time in history because they have at least the capacity to provide a well-balanced source of affirmation, accommodation, moderation, coherence, and synthesis in a pluralistic global community.

References

Audi, Robert. 2004. *The Good and the Right: A Theory of Intuition and Intrinsic Value.* Princeton, NJ: Princeton University Press.

Beauchamp, Thomas and Childress, James. 2000. *Principles of Biomedical Ethics,* Fifth Edition. New York, NY: Oxford University Press.

Churchland, Paul M. 1995. *The Engine of Reason, the Seat of the Soul.* Cambridge, MA: MIT Press.

Corning, Peter. 2003. *Nature's Magic: Synergy in Evolution and the Fate of Humankind.* Cambridge: Cambridge University Press.

Darwin, Charles. 1871. *The Descent of Man, and Selection in Relation to Sex.* 2 vols. London: John Murray.

Eccles, Sir John. 1989. *The Evolution of the Brain: Creation of the Mind.* New York, NY: Routledge.

Erickson, Erik H. 1985. *The Life Cycle Completed.* New York, NY: W. W. Norton.

Hume, David. 1739/1978. *A Treatise of Human Nature.* Oxford: Oxford University.

Inhelder, Barbel and Piaget, Jean. 1958. *The Growth of Logical Thinking: from Childhood to Adolescence.* New York, NY: Basic Books.

James, William. 1907/1975 Pragmatism: *A New Name for Some Old Ways of Thinking.* Cambridge, MA: Harvard University Press.

Kohlberg, Lawrence 1981. *The Philosophy of Moral Development,* vol. I. San Francisco: Harper and Row

Moll, Jorge, et al. April 2002. "The Neural Correlates of Moral Sensitivity," in the *The Journal of Neuroscience.* April 1, 2002, Vol. 27 (7): pp. 2730–2736

Naroll, Raoul. 1983. *The Moral Order.* London: Sage Publications.

Pinker, Steven. 2003. *The Blank Slate: the Modern Denial of Human Nature.* New York, NY: Viking Penguin.

Putnam, Hilaray. 2002. *The Collapse of the Fact/Value Dichotomy.* Cambridge, MA: Harvard University Press.

Quervain, Dominique J.-F. de, et al., August 27, 2004. *Neurobiology of Altruistic Science,* vol. 305: pp. 2354–1258.

Reid, Thomas. 1764/1997. *An Inquiry into the Human Mind on the Principles of Common Sense.* University Park, PA: The Pennsylvania University Press.

Ridley, Matt. 2003. *Nature via Nurture: Genes, Experience, and What Makes Us Human.* New York, NY: Harper Collins.

Rolston, Holmes, III. 1999. *Genes, Genesis and God: Values and Their Origin in Nature and Human History.* Cambridge: Cambridge University Press.

Ross, W. D. 1930. *The Right and the Good.* Oxford: Oxford University Press.

Sagan Carl. 1997. *The Dragons of Eden: Speculations on the Evolutions of Human Intelligence.* New York, NY: Ballantine Books.

Sober, Elliot and Wilson, David Sloan. 1998. *Unto Others: the Evolution and Psychology of Unselfish Behavior.* Cambridge, MA: Harvard University Press.

Stevenson, Leslie. 1987. *Seven Theories of Human Nature.* New York, NY: Oxford University.

Time. May 10, 2004. "What Makes Teens Tick."

Wilson, David Sloan. 2002. *Darwin's Cathedral: Evolution, Religion, and the Nature of Society.* Chicago, IL: University of Chicago Press.

Wilson, Edward O. 1975. *Sociobiology.* Cambridge, MA: Belknap Press.

31

An Ecological Organic Paradigm:
A Framework of Analysis for Moral and Political Philosophy

Levels of Awareness	The Organic Paradigm	McLean (triune brain) +Eccles (neo-neocortex)	Piaget and Kolhberg	Aristotle (Classical Philosophy)	Folk Psychology
Metaphysics	Interpretive Capacity	Neo-Neocortex (with language centers)	Abstract Reasoning	Man Seeks *eudaimonia* (meaning and purpose)	Spiritual
Nature	Reason	Neocortex	Logical Reasoning	Man is a Rational Animal	Mental
Society	Social Conscience	Limbic System	Social Reasoning	Man is a Political (social) Animal	Social
Individual Primal Needs	Appetite	Reptilian Complex	Concrete (self interested) Reasoning	Man is an Animal	Physical

Philosophy (Leslie Stevenson)	Ethics	Law	Principle of Equality	U.S. Constitution (Separation of Powers)	Purposes of Government (Preamble of the U.S. Constitution)
What is the Nature of the Universe? Metaphysics—why?	Deontological (What is obligatory?) (What is my duty?)	Canon Law	Reverence and Reciprocity	Separation of Church and State 1st amendment	Secure Freedom
What is the Nature of the Universe? Natural World—how?	Normative (What is good?)	Roman Law	Reason and Reversiblity	Executive Branch	National Security and Domestic Tranquility (rational order)
What is the Nature of Society?	Communitarian (What is fitting?)	English Common Law	Social Rights and Responsibilities	Judicial Branch	Establish Justice (social justice)
What is the Nature of Man?	Egotistical individual human rights (What is humane?)	Social Contract Theory	Individual Human Rights and the Right to Resist Tyranny	Legislative Branch	Provide for the General Welfare (individual needs)

A current model of pain from the A.M.A.

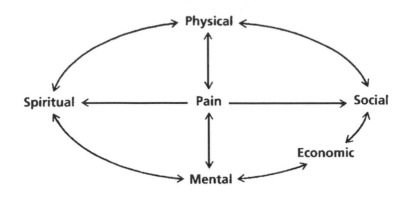

The ship metaphor for a successful expedition

C.S. Lewis (also from classical philosophy)

1. Each ship must be in order and seaworthy
2. The ships need to be able to sail together as a fleet without running into one another or getting separated or lost
3. There must be the knowledge and skill to successfully navigate to the destination
4. There must be a purpose fulfilled by going to the destination or making the journey

Four Principles of Bioethics

1. **Beneficence** — (reciprocity)
   Do unto others, as you would have them
   do unto you — The Golden Rule

2. **Nonmaleficence** — (reversibility)
   Don't do unto others, what you would not want them
   to do unto you — The Silver Rule
   Do no harm

3. **Justice** — (social justice)

4. **Autonomy** — (individual rights)

A graph for analysis
of political philosophies
or political philosophers

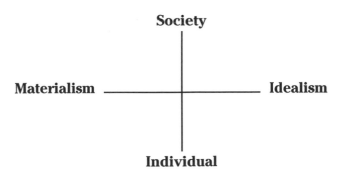

George Orwell

The adjective which is often used to describe George Orwell and his writing is integrity. He was a committed person, an Englishman who fought in the Spanish Civil War against fascism. He was a humanist, but also a writer who was hinged to reality and historical experience. In *Homage to Catalonia,* he wrote of the repercussions of the Stalinist purges of 1936–1938 in Sprain when other socialist writers adhered to the abstract and the ideal. Orwell is best known for *Animal Farm,* a satirical fable on the Russian Revolution, and for the warning of *1984.* He said a lot about the human condition; our dignity, our vulnerability, and our ominous potential for the abuse of power in a technological age.

George Orwell was the pen name of Eric Blair. He was born in 1903 in Imperial India to a lower middle-class family in the Civil Service. He attended boarding school in England at the age of eight *(Such, Such Were the Joys)* and then Eton. From this background, he remained throughout his life very sensitive to the problems of class. He served as a policeman in Burma for five years *(Burmese Days* and *Shooting an Elephant)* and found that he had no taste for authority or imperialism. His disillusionment with capitalism is seen in *The Road to Wigan Pier,* a tour of northern industrial England during the depression.

He became a democratic socialist and this led to his dilemma. During the Spanish Civil War and with the German-Russian Pact, he saw clearly that collectivism, the socialist's hope for improving the lot of the common man, had also the potential to lead to totalitarianism.

Orwell did not abandon democratic socialism, but became the writer who most vividly defined the threat of the totalitarian state to personal freedom. This was the most important issue of his time. Orwell made clear that totalitarianism was a new phenomenon in that, in the name of ideology, it sought to suppress all conflicting sources of authority—church, state, law, culture, education, family and individual spiritual freedom. The ends justified the means. Arthur Koestler, in *Darkness at Noon,* had asserted that unless the means do justice to the ends that ideology is corrupted and indeed changed. Orwell simply stated that imposed ideology is but a thin veil for power for the sake of power. He felt that the totalitarian state was as great a threat to humanity as nuclear warfare.

In *1984,* Orwell explores the malleability of human nature. Marx held that man is only the product of the society in which he lives. In *1984,* Orwell creates a state which attempts through total control of society to change human nature and destroy the personal self. The character of Winston Smith represents cultural values and spiritual freedom and Julia represents instinct and sexual impulse. In the state of Big Brother, however, values and motivation can be inverted. Written on the Ministry of Truth were the three slogans of the Party:

WAR IS PEACE
FREEDOM IS SLAVERY
IGNORANCE IS STRENGTH

In the anti-utopian novel, technology has clearly outstripped moral development. In Huxley's *Brave New World,* social control was through genetic engineering and drugs. In *1984,* it was through brainwashing and terror.

In both *Animal Farm* and *1984,* Orwell emphasizes the importance of language and history. What is important to creating a personal self is culture and tradition; the boring necessities of work and civil duty, and the small pleasures of personal relationships and vegetable gardening.

Oppression begins with the distortion of the truth, therefore candor is one of the burdens of freedom. In *1984,* Newspeak and Doublethink destroy free thought and allow contradiction. History becomes what serves the state, for "who controls the past controls the future; who controls the present controls the past."

In the 1946 essay "Politics and the English Language" Orwell wrote that "in our time, political speech and writing are large-

38

ly the defense of the indefensible. Things...can be defended, but only by arguments which are too brutal for most people to face, and which do not square with the professed aims of political parties...Defenseless villages are bombarded from the air, the inhabitants driven out into the countryside, the cattle machine-gunned, the huts set on fire with incendiary bullets: this is called *pacification*." Orwell had "no capacity for illusion."

One of Orwell's enduring memories of the Spanish War was his inability to shoot an enemy soldier in the early dawn hours who was running along the top of the lines, half dressed, holding his pants up. He was clearly a fellow creature. Orwell makes little of this, but there seems to be the simple recognition that we're all in the same boat, and that without the belt of ideology, we all have to hold our pants up.

Orwell was not a religious person, but in 1944 he wrote, "the real problem is how to restore the religious attitude while accepting death as final." In *Looking Back on the Spanish War*, he wrote, "Privation and brute labour have to be abolished before the real problems of humanity can be tackled. The major problem of our time is the decay of the belief in personal immortality, and it cannot be dealt with while the average human being is either drudging like an ox or shivering in fear of the secret police." In his essay on Charles Dickens he speaks of a cultural unity based on the native decency of people who, although of very different types, can be called the common man. Orwell felt that we should help ameliorate the human condition by being decent to one another.

Recently, Shirley Letwin wrote *The Gentleman in Trollope*, which is a study of individuality and morality in the English character. The integrity of a gentleman's personality, she explains, depends on the coherence of his life, thoughts, and actions. His individuality is not in conflict with his ability to manage his life within a changing communal framework of rules and conventions. Isaiah Berlin wrote in *Russian Thinkers* of the Greek lines of poetry, "The fox knows many things, but the hedgehog knows one big thing." The analogy is that the continental mind has tended toward monistic theories to explain the universe and life, whereas the English, in general, debunk grandiose schemes, see the diversity of human experience, and have a more pragmatic philosophy. It is, for example, the different perspectives of Shakespeare and Dante.

It is in this cultural context that we can best understand Orwell. He was a gentleman and a decent "common" man. Through reflective self-knowledge he valued truth and freedom and extended compassion to others. He was chronically ill with tuberculosis and was dying at the time he wrote *1984*. He was aware of what could be changed and what could not. Throughout his writing he urges us to accept the moral, economic, and political responsibilities of freedom, for he knew how easily freedom could be lost. Philip Rahv said it best when he described Orwell as not merely a friend of mankind but of man.

The Moral Foundations
Of United States Constitutional Democracy

Table of Contents

Originally published in 1992 by Dorrance Publishing Company, Inc.
643 Smithfield Street, Pittsburgh, Pennsylvania 15222

The Moral Foundations
of United States Constitutional Democracy
An Analytical and Historical Inquiry
into the Primary Moral Concept of Equality

The Moral Foundations of United States Constitutional Democracy was written for students of Western civilization and teachers of ethics, law, history, and government. It develops a framework for understanding moral and political philosophy. The framework takes into account several different aspects of human nature and the world in which we live. This provides a basis for understanding several different aspects of universal equality, the unifying "central idea" or primary moral concept of our form of government. The several aspects of universal equality are also traced historically as they developed in different ethical and legal systems of Western civilization. Constitutional democracy in the United States attempts to integrate and balance the several aspects of universal equality as they apply to the coercive powers of government.

I
Introduction

At a time when many nations are throwing off the yokes of totalitarianism and dictatorship it is important that we understand and convey properly the moral foundations of United States constitutional democracy. Those moral foundations at the most fundamental level are not based on capitalism, simple majority-rule democracy, or even freedom. The moral foundations of United States constitutional democracy are based on *several* aspects of universal equality as they relate to the coercive powers of government.

Furthermore, to understand past and current political issues in the United States it is necessary to appreciate that our constitutional democracy is a dynamic system. Our Constitution attempts to incorporate in a pluralistic society several ethical considerations as they relate to the coercive powers of government. This is because the primary concept of

44

equality entails several aspects of human nature and the world in which we live. The Constitution attempts to include several substantive and procedural concepts of equality by first limiting the powers of government and then by dividing and balancing those powers which are delegated to government. Only by referring to the government of the United States as a *constitutional* democracy, however, can we understand and convey to others that it is a dynamic system in which the moral foundations are formed by several aspects of universal equality.

One of the reasons we have some difficulty in understanding the moral foundations of our form of government is that the founding documents presumed that there was a consensus on such matters and therefore do not provide much explanation or commentary. The moral principles and goals of our government, for example, are clearly stated in general terms in the Declaration of Independence and the preamble of the Constitution. *Federalist 39* also makes it clear that the Constitution was meant to be compatible with "the fundamental principles of the Revolution" (Hamilton, Madison, and Jay [1787–88] 1961, 240). The Declaration of Independence, however, describes its primary moral assertion that "all men are created equal" to be a self-evident truth. Later in his life, Thomas Jefferson wrote that the aim of writing the Declaration of Independence was "to place before mankind the common sense of the subject" and he described it as 'an expression of the American mind" with its authority resting on the "harmonizing sentiments of the day" (Foner 1950, 802).

Gary Wills did much to clarify the contemporary usage and meanings of such phrases in his book *Inventing America: Jefferson's Declaration of Independence.* He also concurred, however, with an earlier Jefferson scholar, Douglas Adair, who wrote:

An exact knowledge of Jefferson's ideas...is still lacking.... We know relatively little about his ideas in the context of the total civilization of which he was a part.... Until all of Jefferson's ideas and projects are carefully examined against the back-

> ground of contemporary European developments, and until his theories are appraised as part of the great tradition of Western social thought, we will be unable to take the true measure of the man. (Wills 1979, xxv)

Indeed, the moral assertion that "all men are created equal" has several origins in the Western tradition and derives from several sources of authority which provide the foundations of United States moral, legal, and political thought.

A second reason we have problems understanding both Jefferson and our moral foundations has to do with the English language. Our language has only one word for equality when, in fact, we mean at least four different things by the use of this term in the moral, legal, and political philosophy of Western civilization. As an analog, our language has only one word for love, but the classical Greeks distinguished four different meanings of love with four different words, *epithymeia, eros, philia,* and *agape.* We have a similar problem with the word justice which historically has been closely associated with the concept of equality.

This ambiguity has led to a third problem. As George Orwell observed, totalitarian regimes often distort and invert the truth by corrupting the meaning of words and language. For example, totalitarian communist regimes have, at least in theory, advocated equality as the common ownership of the means of production, but have actually denied political equality as well as the moral agency of other people. Unfortunately, a great deal of intellectual energy has been spent on rebuttal, not by clarifying and defining the *several* aspects of equality and the moral foundations of our *political* system, but in attempts to justify capitalism, distributive justice, inequality, and our economic system in an isolated context.

It would be ironic to accept as a premise of public discourse on constitutional democracy the ideology of Marxism which portrays the economic system to be primary to and determinative of the political system, rather than just an integral and interdependent part of society and government. What is important to recognize is that our economic system, for example the extent to which we are a regulated capitalism or a social welfare state, is determined by constitutional and legislative political processes based on equality. Given such political processes based on equality, it is not irrational for a people to recognize defined property rights, reward production and merit, and incorporate several aspects of distributive justice.

A general *framework* for understanding both the composite and integral aspects of human nature and the world in which we live will be presented and used to help clarify the several different meanings of universal equality. As a tool for understanding, this framework also provides a good reflection of how we have historically defined, understood, and institutionalized the several aspects of universal equality which form the primary moral foundations of United States government.

In 1795, Fisher Ames, a congressman from Massachusetts, perhaps recognized the indeterminate but dynamic aspects of our system of government when he compared it to monarchy in the following way. "A monarchy," he said, "is a merchantman which sails well, but will sometimes strike a rock, and go to the bottom; a republic is a raft which will never sink, but then your feet are always in the water" (Bartlett 1968, 491).

II
Universal Equality
as the Primary Moral Concept

In 1856, before his presidency or the beginning of the Civil War, Abraham Lincoln said:

> Our government rests in public opinion. Whoever can change public opinion, can change the government, practically just so much. Public opinion, or [on?] any subject, always has a "central idea," from which all its minor thoughts radiate. That "central idea" in our political public opinion, at the beginning was, and until recently has continued to be, "the equality of men." (Basler 1953, vol. II, 385; see also Jaffa 1982, chap. XIV)

A few years ago we celebrated the one hundredth anniversary of the Statute of Liberty, and many would consider liberty, or freedom, as the fundamental moral concept on which our government was founded. Freedom, however, has little meaning outside of one's moral concept of justice. Freedom can mean, simply license, the absence of any social obligation or moral constraint. Being a free moral agent does not necessarily mean that one will choose to be moral. Freedom does not address the need to maintain order, establish justice, or provide for the general welfare. Nor does freedom provide much protection from the coercive powers of government unless it means "liberty for all" (Basler 1953, vol. IV, 168–69). Indeed, what we often desire is freedom from the arbitrary will of others.

Morality, on the other hand, provides a context of responsibility for freedom. Morality even implies a degree of freedom of choice and, to the extent of that freedom, responsibility. Freedom by itself implies a type of existential or subjective responsibility but not necessarily any other type of moral acknowledgement. When Jefferson put forth the ideals of our country in the Declaration of Independence, his first assertion, his primary self-evident truth, was that "all men are created equal." The unalienable rights of life, liberty, and the pursuit of happiness were thus put within an ethical context of equality and reciprocity. Jefferson and Lincoln both understood universal equality to be the primary moral concept of American constitutional democracy.

Others have also understood universal equality to be the primary moral concept. Marvin Meyers in his book on James Madison, *The Mind of the Founder,* concluded that, "in Madison's view of man," equality was the fundamental term (1981, xxii). Alexis de Tocqueville, in *Democracy in America* (1835–1840), "advanced the influential thesis that equality is the fundamental theme and characteristic of American civilization" (Davis 1990, 11). Tocqueville noted that even tyrants value freedom, but only for themselves. He also understood that equality is not an extrinsic leveling term but conveys an inherent mutual respect which also implies an equality of political freedom. David Brion Davis, a prominent historian of the institution of slavery, has even concluded that the real anthesis of slavery is not freedom but equality (Davis 1990, 29).

G. K. Chesteron wrote, however, that the belief in human equality is not "some crude fairy tale about all men being equally tall or equally tricky" (see McWilliams 1979,184). It is not like a Procrustean bed of Greek mythology into which all persons are forced to fit by stretching them on a rack or cutting off their legs. For Jefferson, universal equality was instead a moral assertion—an assertion that affirmed both his own humanity and his own individuality against tyranny. Using fable and analogy, in the manner of George Orwell, one could say that if you are a mallard and don't like ducks or duckhood, then there is going to be an inherent problem with your own self-affirmation by definition. This is one sense in which Jefferson's assertion that "all men are created equal" could be considered a self-evident truth. It is an affirmation of our own humanity.

It is this recognition of his own humanity, however, that allowed Jefferson to also assert his own individuality, not by a will to power and coercion, but by inverting that to a resistance to the tyranny of others. By recognizing the moral agency of others, as well as asserting our own mature responsible personality, there opens up the possibility of deciding political issues by the deliberation of democratic constitutional and legislative processes, rather than by simple coercion, domination, or privilege.

The future of American government still rests on public opinion. It rests on our understanding and support for the moral foundations of constitutional democracy and our ability to communicate and preserve such an understand effectively. This is important, for the enjoyment of individual freedom and the progress of human liberty are not inevitable. They are contingent, to a large degree, on our willingness and ability as moral agents to place our free will within ethical constraints. It is indeed the self-imposed ethical or moral foundations of government that change mere obedience to the coercive powers of government into a sense of consensual responsibility for a moral duty, a just order, the common good, or human rights. In United States constitutional democracy these ethical concepts all relate historically to the "central idea" of universal equality.

A Brief Historical Survey of Four Different Aspects of Universal Equality Which Make It an Accommodating or Unifying Moral Concept

Universal equality has several different aspects. It can be arrived at as an ethical concept, an affirmation of our humanity and a moral vision of the world in which we live, from several different directions. This is because there are several different aspects of human nature and several different perspectives of the world in which we live. It is the several aspects of universal equality, however, that make it an accommodating or unifying moral foundation of government in a pluralist society.

Before developing an analytical framework for moral an political philosophy, it will be helpful, as a point of reference, to look at four different aspects of universal equality in the historical context of four different ethical and legal systems. Within Western civilization there developed several sources of moral authority for law and several corresponding ethical and legal systems. Canon Law, Roman Law, English common law, and the social contract theory associated with constitutional law each had a different primary source of moral authority. Each of these systems of law was, consequently, based on a different type of ethical system, and each focused primarily on a different facet of human nature. Constitutional democracy integrates aspects of these four ethical and legal systems as they relate to universal equality and the coercive powers of government.

Canon Law, for example, was based on the authority of God and related primarily to what it understood to be the soul of man. Its ethic is deontological, *deon* meaning "duty" in Greek. That is, it is based on a universal duty "to love God with all thy heart, and with all thy soul, and with all thy strength, and with

50

all thy mind; and thy neighbor as thyself" (Lev 19:18, Deut 6:5, Lk 10:27, Mk 12:29–31). Canon Law contains universal ethical principles based on a reverence for God and reciprocity towards one's fellow man. The equal dignity and worth of all persons in this religious system derives from a belief that God not only created humanity, but that man and woman were also made in God's image (Gen 1:27). Equality is intrinsic and not derived from one's individual attributes, but from the relationship between God and humanity.

Roman Law, on the other hand, incorporated significant aspects of natural law based on the authority of a perceived natural moral order in the universe. Such a natural moral order could be understood by all persons, it was believed, because all humans share a capacity for right reason, an ability to know right from wrong. All of the various people within the vast Roman empire, for example, could be expected to learn and know that is wrong to steal. The ethical system of natural law is primarily normative (based on norms or ideals). Universal equality in classical civilization is based on all human beings having a capacity for right reason and also on a concept of reversibility which requires a rational imagination and empathy.

Aristotle, in his *Poetics,* described reversibility as one of two major elements in Greek tragedies. The second element is catharsis, part of which is a realization that we all, even heroes and kings, have character flaws and are also subject to fate, both of which can lead to a reversal of fortunes. An ethic based on reversibility is not just archaic. In the first century, Rabbi Hillel taught, "What is hateful to thyself do not do to another. This is the whole Law, the rest is commentary" (Shab. 31a). It is also the basis, however, of the Kantian categorical imperative that one cannot place oneself outside of morality without implicity permitting others to do the same. Reversibility was also a primary moral reason in the thought of both Jefferson and Lincoln in their opposition to slavery (Basler 1953, vol. II, 532; Jefferson [1785] 1972, 163). The more recent concept of John Rawls in *A Theory of Justice* (1971) of justice as fairness, with an original position in which one does not know either his or her fate or circumstances in life's game, is an extension of the concept of reversibility.

Common law in English feudal society derived its moral authority from yet another source—not from God or nature, but from social custom and tradition. This was primarily a communitarian ethical system. It related to the social conscience of the people based on their ethical concepts of rights and responsibilities in society. Traditional English rights progressively became a basis of communal solidarity.

Finally, the social contract theory associated with constitutional law derives its moral authority beginning with the individual in a state of nature concerned primarily about his own safety and happiness. Its very premise is not only that all are free and equal in a state of nature but that everyone is also endowed with natural rights which they are entitled to defend. Such a theory is based on individual concerns and contract. The universality of social contract theory as it applies to democratic processes and constitutional law, however, makes it essentially a humanitarian ethic. It contains an ethic of universal equality based on what we now refer to as human rights and a just claim to resist the violation of those rights.

American constitutional democracy integrates and balances these four ethical systems as they apply to the several aspects of universal equality and the coercive powers of government. The accommodating common moral concept is not just a deontological ethic, with concepts of reverence and reciprocity, relating to God and a person's soul; nor is it just a normative ethic based on concepts of right reason and reversibility, relating to a perceived moral order in nature and our capacity to understand that order with our reason; nor is it just a communitarian ethic, with concepts of social rights and responsibilities, as they relate to the several aspects of society and our social conscience; nor is it only a humanitarian ethic, with a concept of human rights and the right to resist tyranny, relating to our individual lives and our fundamental needs and desires. The accommodating or unifying moral concept is universal equality which can be derived analytically, and has been derived historically, from each of these sources of authority and aspects of human nature.

III
An Analytical Framework for Moral and Political Philosophy

A general analytical framework for moral and political philosophy, which incorporates four aspects of human nature and relates them as cognitive modes to four aspects of the world in which we live, can now be developed with this brief historical context in mind. Evolutionary theory, for example, postulates such a developmental interaction between an organism and its environment. Evolutionary theory aside, however, an interaction between human nature and the world in which we live is also a very practical matter. In *Jurisprudence: Principles and Applications,* for example, Ervin H. Pollack distinguishes between philosophy in theory and philosophy in practice. Concerning the latter he states that "The criteria from which we study the world and its relationships are derived from the world itself" (1979, xiv).

For the purpose of general analysis, four aspects of human nature or roughly four capacities or cognitive modes at which our minds function, will be considered. These are appetite (which relates to our primal needs and desires), social conscience, reason, and interpretation. The premise is that our moral thought is not unlike the development of our other mental behavior. It begins, like the cognitive development of the child, with concrete thinking, and progresses to social concepts, logical reasoning and finally abstract concepts of meaning and purpose which also serve an integrating and narrative function. (This is in part a modification on the work of Lawrence Kohlberg in *The Philosophy of Moral Development: Moral Stages and the Idea of Justice* [1981], which itself is based on the work of Jean Piaget.)

In Western civilization, these four aspects of human nature or cognitive modes have been loosely associated with our need to deal with several aspects or perspectives of the world

53

in which we live. The four mental capacities or cognitive modes are loosely associated with our own individual primal needs and desires, with society, with the natural world in which we live, and with metaphysicial or religious questions. The premise here is that our mental capacities develop in response to a corresponding and widening field of experience or perception of reality concerning the world in which we live. For example, our appetite relates to our individual primal needs and desires, our conscience to our social relationships, our logical reasoning relates primarily to the natural world in which we live, and our capacity for interpretation relates to our need to deal with metaphysical or religious questions.

One is tempted to relate this progressive cognitive development also to a model of the evolution of brain structure described by Paul MacLean as the *triune brain* (Sagan 1977, 57–83; Konner 1983, 147–152). The triune brain is a model for the progressive evolutionary development of three layers of the forebrain which MacLean believes can still be distinguished neuroanatomically and functionally in our own brain structure. He describes first a "reptilian complex" which surrounds the midbrain and which probably evolved several hundred million years ago. It relates to such primal instincts as sex and aggression. This is surrounded by a limbic system which is fully developed in mammals but not in reptiles. This he relates to emotions and a social capacity other than primal hierarchy. Surrounding the rest of the brain is the neocortex, which in humans makes up about eighty-five percent of the brain and is associated with reason. To this model one could easily add, at least functionally, the language centers in the left hemisphere of the brain and the capacity for abstract thinking which includes interpretation as integration and narrative.[1] Also, the concept of the evolution and development of capacities rather than anatomical levels is more appropriate, for the brain is a very dynamic structure and highly integrated from top to bottom.

Without obscure anatomical detail and from introspection alone, however, we are aware that we tend to integrate our accumulated thoughts, feelings, and actions into a sense of identity or self and interpretive narrative concepts of orientation and meaning. It is also apparent that we interact with other people and our environment, though never with complete certainty and sometimes not even very well. On the one hand, it is easily demonstrated that our minds affect our perception of reality. Two people, for example, may see the very same thing quite differently. On the other hand, St. Thomas Aquinus and others have felt that the mind also conforms to reality. For the purpose of *general* analysis, the framework I am proposing loosely relates four capacities or modes of cognition of our composite and integral nature to four different aspects of the world in which we live. It is the extreme complexity of human nature, our relations to the world, and the course of history that make such categories useful as a *framework* for understanding.[2]

The general analytical framework I am proposing and will apply to our concepts of universal equality and constitutional democracy can also be seen, in this context, to be derived from the work of Leslie Stevenson, a Lecturer in Logic at the University of St. Andrews. It is a modification of the method of analysis he uses in *Seven Theories of Human Nature* (1987). He maintains that the best way to understand the ideas of any political philosophy or philosopher is to consider the underlying assumptions concerning the nature of the universe, the nature of society, and the nature of man. Since the Copernican revolution, however, Western civilization has tended to separate questions concerning the nature of the universe into those of science, relating to the natural world in which we live, and those of metaphysics and religion, relating to our broader interpretation of identity, orientation, and meaning.[3] The analytical framework proposed here, therefore, would consider assumptions related to four rather than three aspects of the world in which we live, to include metaphysical as well as scientific concepts of the universe. Corresponding to this, the analytical framework also considers four modes of cognition to include the interpretive, integrative, and narrative aspect of thought (which relates to metaphysics), as well as the more immediate, logical processing and calculating component of reasoning (which relates more to science and the natural world in which we live).

For the purpose of general analysis, again, the framework I am proposing relates four capacities or modes of recognition of our composite and integral nature (appetite, conscience, reason, and interpretation) to four aspects of the world in which we live (our own individual primal needs and desires, society, nature, and metaphysical aspects of the universe). This analytical framework is important for its reflects on how we have defined, understood, and institutionalized the *several* moral aspects of universal equality.

It is understood that our categories of thought are significantly influenced by our culture and language. It is also understood that, from an anthropological standpoint, most societies have been based on tradition and kinship-descent lines and without formal written laws. Still other societies have been what Max Weber (1864–1920) described as charismatic in the source of their legitimation and organization (Weber [1921] 1964, 328). From an anthropological viewpoint, what Weber calls legally-based societies have been relatively few. Pluralistic societies based on law are almost an exception. Yet, it is in legal systems and the language of law that our own particular historical ethical traditions and theories have been brought to action or limitation of action concerning the coercive powers government.

IV
The Several Aspects of Universal Equality as They Relate to the Moral Authority of Law, the Coercive Powers of Government, Integration, and Constitutional Democracy

The Moral Authority of Constitutional Democracy is Based on Both "Higher Law" Concepts of Equality and Democratic Procedural Concepts of Equality

The moral authority and legitimacy of law, corresponding with this analytical framework, can be based on metaphysics or religion, on nature, on some aspect of society, or on the individual. In Western civilization we have developed "higher law" concepts of authority based primarily on Judaic and Christian monotheism and the concept of natural law which was developed in classical civilization. These "higher law" sources of moral authority are not dependent on either our social or our individual will. The following description of natural law was derived primarily from Stoic philosophy by Cicero:

> There is in fact a true law—namely, right reason—which is in accordance with nature, applies to all men, and is unchangeable and eternal. By its commands this law summons men to the performance of their duties, by its prohibitions it restrains them from doing wrong. Its commands and prohibitions always influence good men but are without effect upon the bad. To invalidate this law by human legislation is never morally right, nor is it permissible ever to restrict its operation, and to annul it wholly is impossible. Neither the senate nor the people can absolve us from our obligation to obey this law, and it requires no Sextus Aelius to expound and interpret it. It will not lay down one rule at Rome and another at Athens, nor will it be one rule to-day and another to-morrow. But there will be one law, eternal and unchangeable, binding at all times upon all peoples; and there will be, as it were, one common master and ruler of men, namely God, who is the author of this law, its interpreter, and its sponsor. The man who will not obey it will abandon his better self, and, in denying the true nature of man, will thereby suffer the severest of penalties though he has escaped all the other consequences which men call punishments. (Sabine and Thorson 1973, 161–2)

The concepts of universal equality in "higher law" tend to be intrinsic and qualitative such as the dignity and worth of the individual.

Western civilization also developed concepts of law in which society and the individual serve as the source of moral authority and legitimacy. Examples of these would be the socially-based communitarian common law of English feudal society and its reinterpretation as social contract theory based on the free and equal individual in a state of nature.

Rights and responsibilities in feudal societies were based on status and tradition, but they were also of a contractual nature. Universal equality in contractual concepts of law tends to be quantitative and numerical, as in a utilitarian ethic, or as in government by consent with one person, one vote, which is the basis of the democratic process. These are basically procedural concepts of equality.

Constitutional democracy combines qualitative, substantive, "higher law" concepts of justice and universal equality derived primarily from classical civilization and Judeo-Christian religion with quantitative, procedural concepts of justice and equality derived primarily from the communitarian ethic of common law, republican traditions, and social contract theory. Thus, universal equality is both the fundamental qualitative moral principle of our system of government and the basis of the fundamental quantitative democratic process by which it was ordained and ratified, and by which it functions. These different aspects of universal equality were partially reconciled by a democratic constitutional process in which the sovereign people verified a commitment of certain qualitative or substantive "higher law" concepts of equality as they relate to the coercive powers of government. Furthermore, they required a super-majority for any subsequent amendment of these principles in our constitutional law.

The fundamental law of the land, except for the possibility of another constitutional convention, is placed beyond the reach of a simple majority. That is, two-thirds of the Congress and three-fourths of the states are required to amend the principles in the Constitution. To this extent, however, even the choice of those principles to be included in American constitutional law rests on public opinion.[4]

Government as Coercive Power and Its Limitation and Regulation by the Constitution as a Social Contract Based on Equality

What distinguishes moral philosophy as it applies to political philosophy is that government is communal and it concerns primarily the use of coercive power. Taxation is essentially a coercive power. In addition, one of the purposes of government is to ensure social order and thus remove individuals from an escalating cycle of personal revenge. Government, in one view, can be considered a monopoly of coercive power (Weber [1921] 1964, 154). The problem then becomes not only the moral authority of government, but also the limitation and regulation of its coercive power.

One of the strengths of what historian Adrienne Koch called the *great collaboration* between Jefferson and Madison was that between them they had a balanced appreciation of both the possibilities and the limitations of human nature and our capacity for self-government (Koch 1964). The political philosophy which underlies the founding documents thus reflects a concern for both the moral foundations of government and for the limitation and regulation of governmental power. The Constitution, which incorporates this political philosophy, was perceived to be a social contract, a fundamental law of the land which was ordained and ratified by the people. The concept of government as a social contract, however, has not always led to the limitation and regulation of governmental power.

Writing at the time of the Puritan Revolution and civil war, Thomas Hobbes (1588–1679) had argued in *Leviathan* (1651) that sovereignty is not based on divine right or even a *summum bonum,* a highest good, but on the ability and power to establish order. Whatever "Mortall God" could impose order on man's natural state of "warre of every man against every man" had and deserved the implied sovereignty of the people. This "Mortall God" could also define justice and law where previously there had been none. In the state of nature, as perceived by Hobbes, all persons are equal in that they fear a violent death and they are all not only capable of killing one another but are also free to do so. With such a pessimistic view of human nature, Hobbes had the state establish order (chap. 13). In contrast, Jean Jacques Rousseau (1712–1778), writing at a time prior to the French Revolution, had an ambiguous but optimistic view of humanity in a state of nature. Theories based on his writings would later attempt to have the state also define morality, not by simple imposition but by associating it with the concept of the general will. Revolutionary movements in continental Europe—from aspects of the French Revolution to the Russian Revolution, from Communism to Fascism—were based on such unlimited concepts of all order and morality being defined by the state.

John Locke (1632–1704) had a more moderate concept of humanity in the state of nature, and therefore a more moderate concept of the social contract and the role of government. He considered individual rights to precede the formation of government. He reasoned from that premise that society could place limits on the coercive powers of government or even change the government by revolution for good cause. The concept of a social contract as the authority for government served Locke's purposes well. By placing all sovereignty in the people, rather than relying on a constitutional tradition of mixed government that included the king, Locke was able to provide a rational foundation for government by consent, parliamentary supremacy, and the Glorious Revolution of 1688.

Thomas Paine, in *Common Sense* (1776), also used the concept of the social contract. He felt that the mutual benefits and concerns of society in a state of nature preceded government. He also recognized government as a coercive power, however, and he wrote that "Government, even in its best state, is a necessary evil, in its worse state, an intolerable one" (Paine [1776] 1982, 65). Before Paine, the thirteen colonies had focused their grievances mainly on England's Parliament. The Parliament had both violated traditional principles of constitutional law and denied the colonies representation which stood for the concept of self-government. In addition, Paine attacked the king, the whole concept of monarchy, and thus solidarity with England. Locke's arguments for legitimate revolution and popular sovereignty were now brought to bear against the whole government of England, both the Parliament and the king. Paine argued for declaring independence and called for a

"Continental Conference" to form a "Charter of the United Colonies." "But where, say some, is the King of America?", he wrote, and he answered, "...that so far as we approve of monarchy, that in America THE LAW IS KING" (Paine [1776] 1982, 96–98). American government was to be constitutional, or in the words of Chief Justice John Marshall in *Marbury v. Madision* (1803), "a government of laws, and not of men." Government was to represent the people not just in theory; it was to be accountable to a fundamental law of the land ordained and ratified by the people and to a democratic process.

The American development of constitutional democracy formally combined the earlier medieval English concept of government as limited by law and the concept of government by consent. Our constitution was originally perceived to have moral authority both because it contained "higher law" concepts of freedom, equality, and justice *and* because it was ordained and ratified by the people (Corwin 1955,4). Because the sovereignty of the people was formally expressed in a written constitution and the supreme Court was given a power of judicial review, neither parliamentary supremacy nor monarchy established themselves in the United States. Through a constitutional process certain principles and values were placed even beyond the reach of transient legislative majorities. It is our Constitution that both limits and divides governmental power and gives it political accountability on the basis of several aspects of equality.[5]

Moderation and Integration by Balancing the Several Different Aspects of Universal Equality

United States constitutional democracy begins with some of the same premises as the classical Greek philosophers, and yet it reaches somewhat different conclusions. Similar to the philosophy of Aristotle, for example, it does assume that man is a political animal, meaning that people naturally desire to live in a *polis,* or community. However, unlike Aristotle, who divided the world into Greeks and barbarians, our form of government gives more recognition to the universal aspects of the human community. Indeed, it was not Aristotle, but his pupil, Alexander the Great, who developed the concept of *homonoia,* meaning concord, as a practical matter of developing unity within his diverse and pluralistic empire. It was also during this period of Hellenism that the Stoics developed more fully the concept of a moral law of nature which all persons could understand by their shared capacity for right reason. The Stoics also superseded the perspective of the Greek city-state with the concept of the cosmopolitan, meaning citizen of the universe.

Also similar to the classical Greek political philosophers, our form of government recognizes both the composite nature of human beings and the need for moderation. The teaching of Socrates had been to "know yourself." Plato in his description of justice taught that you should also be true to yourself, especially as to what is your particular merit and what you deserve or is your due. Aristotle was the philosopher of temperance, moderation, and the "golden mean." Of course, if you really know yourself, and are really truthful or honest with yourself and about what you deserve, then it becomes obvious why we should all act with some moderation.

Each of these classical Greek philosophers, however, to a greater or lesser degree attempted to achieve such harmony and moderation in the individual and in society on the basis of reason, which they considered the highest function of human beings (Nagel 1972).[6] United States constitutional democracy attempts instead to achieve accommodation and moderation in a pluralistic society first by limiting the powers of government and then by applying a system of checks and balances to the different functions of government, rather than creating a hierarchy based on intelligence, religion, class, power, tradition, or paternalism. Universal equality achieves some moderation when the concept of the dignity and worth of the individual is understood as a matter which requires the consideration and balancing of at least four different capacities and perspectives. It is important to recognize, however, that this moderation by balancing, which constitutional democracy attempts to achieve, does not portray or understand such ethical questions as *What is obligatory?*, *What is good?*, *What is fitting?*, or *What is humane?* to be based only on material considerations of utility, simply arbitrary, totally relative, or merely subjective. This differs from situational ethics in that all the considerations remain grounded in the concept of universal equality and concern primarily the coercive powers of government.

Within this analytical framework, it is understandable that there are particular consequential ethical considerations as well as more abstract, universal metaphysical obligations and values. On the other hand, it is understandable that particular facts, or what we believe to be facts, are not the sole determinants of values. Moral obligations are not always the same as the positive laws of the state. Natural rights or human rights are not the same as just unfettered individualism. Yet, there remain valid natural, social, individual, and even transcendental claims if persons affirm themselves and their humanity, the premise of community, and a concept of continuity.

In this framework of analysis, integration is concerned internally with a reconciliation of our mind's four capacities of interpretation, reason, conscience, and appetite. External integration relates to a reconciliation of our metaphysical ideas, our relation to the world in which we live, our relation to society, and our own individual self-interest. This is perhaps better understood by examining the opposite concept of alienation. Discord and alienation often result when one of our levels of understanding is emphasized to the exclusion of the others, or when, as a society, we develop ideologies that relate to one of our concepts of metaphysics, nature, society, or human beings, but to the exclusion of the other three. In a pluralistic society, there is a potential political problem when only one aspect of human nature is emphasized or when any aspect of human nature is excluded or not taken into consideration. The importance of the concept of alienation in Western civilization can be seen in two of its major systems of belief. Monotheism considers sin to be alienation from God and one's fellow human beings. Marxism considers the problem of capitalism to be man's alienation from himself.

The Institutionalization of the Several Concepts of Universal Equality In United States Constitutional Democracy

In attempting to achieve integration or accommodation on the basis of equality, our system of government does leave the question of meaning and purpose to the individual. This is what Jefferson, following Aristotle, meant by the "pursuit of happiness," which is quite different from the pursuit of pleasure as we understand it. The level of function that interprets, integrates, and narrates meaning, purpose, and continuity in our lives, and deals with the ultimate questions of metaphysics and religion, is separated from the coercive powers and structure of government. Historically, this developed first in Western civilization as both conflict and the sharing of powers between church and state, then as a doctrine of religious toleration in England, and finally as both the disestablishment of religion and the freedom of religion from the coercive powers of government in the United States of America.

Individual conscience is protected and it remains, of course, reflected in our culture, our public opinion, and in our government policies. The individual moral personality is, in fact, the basis of both our constitutional principles and democratic processes. The free and equal individual with moral responsibility is the basis of communal solidarity. The stated general purposes of our Constitution can thus be both to form a more perfect union *and* to secure the blessings of liberty to ourselves and our posterity.

The powers that are delegated to government are divided into executive, judicial, and legislative functions, which are then integrated by checks and balances rather than by placing them in a hierarchy of order. The separation of powers is a fundamental part of the Constitution. The different functions of these divisions of government to make, adjudicate, and enforce the law are somewhat analogous to the specific stated purposes of government in the Constitution to promote the general welfare, establish justice, and maintain security and domestic tranquility. Each division of government, therefore, has a different function and a different primary moral concern as well as a duty to uphold the entire Constitution. Each is also institutionally accountable to constitutional principles and democratic processes based on equality.

The different divisions and functions of our government remain to some extent connected historically to ethical and legal structures which relate to our capacities of reason, conscience, and appetite and our need to deal with nature (unity and order), society (social justice), and our own individual interests (general welfare). The older organic metaphor of the body politic can still be recognized. We still, for example, refer to the chief executive as the "head" of state. The divisions of government in classical and medieval mixed governments were by social class. The divisions of government in United States constitutional democracy are by function and they are accountable to principles and processes based on equality. In addition, however, none of the functions and moral purposes of our divisions of government are by themselves determinate.

It can easily be argued that the accommodating concepts of constitutional democracy are the basis of American pragmatism. Our government recognizes not only the wisdom of a separation of powers, but also a dynamic of ethical considerations. It attempts to achieve a workable and functional accommodation and unity of these considerations in a pluralistic society on the basis of several aspects of equality.

V
A Historical Perspective
Medieval Limitations on the Coercive Powers of Government

The predominant idea or orientation in the Middle Ages was not *equality* but *hierarchy*. The concept of the universe as a great hierarchical chain of being had its origin primarily in classical Greek philosophy (Lovejoy 1936, 24). The concept of hierarchy, however, can also be easily seen in Judeo-Christian religion and the military, economic, and social structure of feudal society, which was predominantly Germanic and pagan in origin. These were the major elements that went into the crucible of the Middle Ages in Europe which formed Western civilization. It is not such a paradox, therefore, that they are also the primary sources of our concepts of equality. In our colonial experience, religion was Christian, education was classical and the legal system was English and based on feudal common law dating back to the Magna Charta.

As described in the brief historical preface, each of the three major ethical and legal systems that formed Western civilization at the time of the Middle Ages focused on a different aspect of human nature and perspective of the world in which we live. The ethical principles of universal equality are based on a universal moral duty of reverence and reciprocity in Judeo-Christian religion, on reason and reversibility in classical civilization, and on communal rights and responsibilities in the military, economic, and social relationships of Anglo-Saxon feudal structures. These also represent primarily deontological (based on duty), normative (based on norms or ideals), and communitarian (based on social tradition) ethical systems.

Both the natural law of classical civilization and Judeo-Christian monotheism had a concept of an order in the universe which placed the free will of human beings in a moral context. Throughout classical Greek literature, for example, there is a recognition that tyranny, excessive pride (hubris), and revenge lead to discord and tragedy. Correspondingly, throughout Judaic and Christian scripture there is the recognition that shalom (pease, wholeness, and harmony) depends not only on justice but also on atonement and forgiveness which lead to reconciliation. *Shalom, Islam,* and *salvation* all have either similar etymological roots (SLM) or meanings. The communitarian ethic of English society, originally based on custom and tradition, is somewhat unique in that it developed into a concept of rights for the free and equal individual with moral responsibility as the basis of communal solidarity. Custom and tradition are often given some of the validity of natural law concepts in so far as they represent the accumulated "right reason" of the community. These structured ethical systems developed into the legal structures of Roman Law, Canon Law and common law which in the Middle Ages restricted the coercive powers of government.

This general framework in no way denies that the three major sources of Western civilization were certainly mixed ethical systems and also based, at least in the Middle Ages, on a concept of hierarchy. The concept of the moral authority of law deriving from the individual citizen would achieve prominence only later in the development of the modern state and constitutional democracy.

The Authority for Law Based on the Individual and Government by Consent

Our concept of the authority of law also being based on the morally responsible individual, government by consent, and the democratic process required a revolution in the hierarchical thought of the Middle Ages. Nevertheless, these concepts also had their origins in the democratic and republican traditions of Greece and Rome, in the Judeo-Christian concepts of covenant and compact, and in the Germanic traditions of election and contract. A revolution occurred in religion during the Reformation. A revolution in social, economic and cultural affairs occurred during the Renaissance. The scientific revolution changed the perceptions of both nature and cosmology and culminated in the Enlightenment. Each of these contributed to a revolution in thought which gave impetus to the notion of the individual, and his safety and happiness, being the basis of authority for government.

The Reformation challenged hierarchy within the church. Martin Luther developed the concepts of the priesthood of all believers and the stewardship of all callings or vocations to God. He also translated the Bible into German placing an

67

emphasis on literacy. The Calvinist reformers developed democratic and representative forms of church government. Yet, the Presbyterian Samuel Rutherford in *Lex Rex* (1644) could argue for political equality under the Calvinist doctrine of original sin that all are equally depraved. A king, he wrote, "is under the same state of sin... of which he hath a share equally with all other men by nature... And if there be none a king by nature, there can be none a subject by nature" (Lakoff 1964, 61). The religious wars and persecutions forced the issue of religious pluralism within a political unity and eventually led to policies of toleration and freedom of conscience.

During the Renaissance, a philosophy of humanism developed the concept of the dignity and worth of the individual. The medieval unity based on hierarchy was also challenged by a revival of interest in classical civilization, a greater concern for individual education and development, a method of critical thought, secular concepts of the state, occasional republican forms of government, and a spirit of liberty. Greater social recognition was given to the arts and to the active life, to exploration and capitalism.

The other major influence challenging a tradition of hierarchy was the scientific revolution. The implications of the cosmology of Copernicus and its challenge to accepted authority are evident in the trial of Galilleo. René Descartes challenged the basis of all knowledge with his system of radical doubt, which led to the subjective "I think, therefore I am." This was a search for certainty which also placed man back at the center of the universe, or at least at the center of a theory of knowledge. Perhaps more significant to the revolution in thought, however, was the development of empirical inductive thought and experimentation as a method to verify and compliment rational deductive thought and contemplation. A growing understanding of nature and the ability to use that knowledge lead to a greater concern with this world and secular matters. Knowledge, which had previously been understood as virtue, came to be understood as power.

James I, who was also the head of the Church of England,

68

understood the political interconnection of these forms of revolutionary thought when he said "no bishop, no king" (Roberts, C. and Roberts, D. 1980, 328). The challenge to hierarchy as a mode of thought or paradigm was, indeed, best captured subsequently by a description of the more radical aspects of the Puritan Revolution as "the world turned upside down" (Hill 1975). In English feudal history, the Magna Charta was an aristocratic document, but it had egalitarian implications. By the time of the Puritan Revolution, Colonel Rainborough, a spokesman for the Levellers, would declare in the Putney debates:

> For really I think that the poorest he that is in England hath a life to live, as the greatest he; and therefore truly, sir, I think it clear, that every man that is to live under a government ought first by his own consent to put himself under that government; and I do think that the poorest he in England is not at all bound in the strict sense to that government that he hath not had a voice to put himself under. (Lakoff 1964, 67)

A Transition in Constitutional Theory— Coke and Locke

A major transitional figure in constitutional theory was Sir Edward Coke. Coke was at the center of the struggle to prevent the first Stuart king, James I, from using the royal prerogative and the concept of the divine right of kings to interfere with the constitutional law of England and traditional English rights (Corwin, 1955; Roberts, C. and Roberts, D. 1980, chap. 13). Coke represents a shift in the relationship between "higher law" concepts of authority and the authority of procedural democratic concepts of law.

In his *Second Institutes* and as a judge and eventually chief justice of the King's Bench, Coke attempted to extend the "common right and reason" of natural law and common law to include procedural concepts of due process (Forkosch 1973). In *Dr. Bonham's* Case (1610), for example, he stated that the Royal College of Physicians, which had been incorporated by Parliament, could not act as judges, ministers, and the recipients of fines. In what was to become known as Coke's Dictum he declared an Act of Parliament void:

> One cannot be judge in his own case.... And it appears in our books that in many cases the common law will control Acts of Parliament, and sometimes adjudge them to be utterly void. For when an Act of Parliament is against common right and reason, or repugnant, or impossible to be performed, the common law will control it and adjudge such an Act to be void.

In *Calvin's Case* (1608), he stated, "the law of nature cannot be changed or taken away" and "should direct this case." Coke's Dictum has been considered the single most important source of what became in American constitutional law the concept of judicial review.

In 1616, after pleading independence of the judiciary in cases involving the king, Coke was dismissed from the bench. He was subsequently, however, elected to Parliament in 1621. There he used the Magna Charta as fundamental law to defend the rights of Parliament, and Parliament as a court, to in turn define and defend the fundamental law. As a member of Parliament, Coke was a major force in developing the Petition of Rights which declared unparliamentary taxation, billeting of troops, arbitrary imprisonment, and martial law over civilians all to be illegal. Coke was now using basically representative procedural methods to validate concepts of due process and traditional English rights.

Sir Edward Coke helped to define and defend the concept of constitutional law, the concept of a fundamental law of the land. There is a progression which extends from the Magna Charta, the Petition of Rights, and the English Bill of Rights of 1689, to the Bill of Rights in the United States Constitution. Our own constitutional process affirmed and politically validated what were believed to be certain "higher law" principles.

A new synthesis and unity of thought developed in the later part of the seventeenth century based on Isaac Newton's laws of nature (Randall 1926, chap. XI). The concept was that of an orderly mechanical universe, with the metaphor being that of a clock and God as the clock maker. John Locke used such a concept of nature and God to convert "higher law" concepts into those of the natural rights of the free and equal individual in a state of nature. Locke's natural rights include life, liberty, and property and he intermingled these somewhat by stating that one has a property in his own person. In the social contract of Locke, limited powers are delegated to government because there is a need to define, adjudicate, and enforce laws to protect both society and the safety of the individual. Government, however, is by consent.[7] Society has a right, therefore, to overthrow a government that abuses its delegated powers.

Locke is a transitional figure because he helped change the metaphor or paradigm by which we understand political philosophy. His major political work was entitled *Two Treatises on Government* (1690). In the first treatise he disassembled patriarchy, the prevailing metaphor for hierarchy in both the family and government. In his more famous second treatise, Locked used the concept of a social contract between free and equal individuals in a state of nature to translate theistic and natural law concepts into the language of natural rights for the individual. In the second treatise the individual is perceived to not only have natural rights but also to be the source of authority for government.

The Integration of Ethical Traditions— Kant, Jefferson, and Lincoln

William Barrett, in *The Death of the Soul,* considers Immanual Kant (1724–1804) to be "the last great thinker in whom the intellectual unity of the Western mind is still held together" (1986, 52). There are some parallels in his formulations of the categorical imperative (the universal rule) to metaphysical, natural law, communitarian and individual considerations. Treating human beings as an end and not as a means, for example, could be considered to be a normative ethic as well as a deontological ethic. Kant also, however, subscribed to a new type of dualism in separating the knower

71

from that which is known. We cannot know a thing in itself, he claimed, but only our perception of it. St. Augustine's theology and philosophy had been self-reflective. Kant's theology and philosophy, however, became self-referential. Kant's concept of morality is based on universal equality but, because his epistemology separates the knower from that which is known, it is not externally integrated. It is based on the rational individual as moral agent without concessions to God, nature, or a society of other moral agents.

I perceive a more satisfactory unity and integration of metaphysics, nature, social theory, and the nature of human beings in the eclectic moral thought of Thomas Jefferson. Jefferson's thought included Stoic, Christian, humanist, deist, and moral sense philosophy, but it also included Epicurean, utilitarian, agrarian, Enlightenment, social contract, and natural rights concepts (Koch 1943). God, nature, society, and individuals, however, were still all included in a pragmatic system that both understood a person to be a free and responsible moral agent and also was based on a concept of universal equality.

Both Kant and Jefferson had an intellectual span that was able to incorporate both the particular and the universal. Kant is perhaps seen as the culmination of the Enlightenment in that he was able to expand his self-referential reasoning from the particular to universal conclusions. Jefferson, on the other hand, often beginning with universals and self-evident truths, was able to relate them to the individual moral personality. Kant lived his entire life in the small town of Königsberg in East Prussia, yet he is credited with being among the first to postulate that there were other universes, other galaxies than our own. Jefferson,who is more correctly viewed as the beneficiary of a diverse humanist tradition, was a prime example of what we think of as a Renaissance man—broad, diverse, and international in his thought and actions. Yet, in an addendum to his autobiography, he wrote that he thought that the most important contribution a person could make was to introduce a new plant to his native soil (Koch 1943, 190; Padover 1943, 1288).

Kant, in his own thought, separated theology from empirical

knowledge. Jefferson, on the other hand, was instrumental in separating religion from the coercive power of government. Jefferson understood that one of his most important works was the Statute of Virginia for Religious Freedom.

Though one can easily find fault with Jefferson and some of his writings, it is very important to understand that for him the self-evident truth that "all men are created equal" was a universal moral assertion. Jefferson felt that nature was the work of a God who was "Nature's God," the Architect, the Creator, the First Cause. Human beings were in this sense created equal. They are also equal he felt in that they are "endowed by their Creator with certain unalienable rights" which include "life, liberty, and the pursuit of happiness." Indeed, it was to secure these rights associated with the moral assertion of universal equality that "Governments are instituted amongst men, deriving their just powers from the consent of the governed." The Declaration of Independence is argued in the manner of Euclidean geometry. It is also significant to note in this context that, unlike Locke, Jefferson did not include property in his first principles or axioms.

More specifically, Jefferson felt that we all share equally a common humanity in that we have a capacity for, and possess, a moral sense (Padover 1943, 1032–34). In a letter to his young friend Peter Carr, Jefferson wrote:

He who made us would have been a pitiful bungler, if he had made the rules of our conduct a matter of science. For one man of science, there are a thousand who are not. What would have become of them? Man was destined for society. His morality, therefore, was to be formed to this object. He was endowed with a sense of right and wrong merely relative to this. This sense is as much a part of his nature, as the sense of hearing, seeing, feeling; it is the true foundation of morality.... The moral sense, or conscience, is as much a part of man as his leg or his arm. It is given to all human beings in a stronger or weaker degree.... It may be strengthened by exercise, as may any particular limb of the body. This sense is submitted, indeed in some degree, to the guidance of reason; but it is a small stock which is required for this; even a less one that what we call Common sense. State a moral case to a ploughman and a professor. The former will decide it as well, and often better than the latter, because he has not been led astray by artificial rules. (Peterson 1977, 424)

Jefferson's respect for the moral agency of others was indeed an affirmation of his own humanity, a self-affirmation. Concerning women he wrote, "It is civilization alone which replaces women in the enjoyment of their natural equity. That first teaches us to subdue the selfish passions, and to respect those rights in others that we respect in ourselves" (Jefferson [1785] 1972, 60). Jefferson was opposed to religious, political, and social tyranny; thus, equality for him was also a matter of self-assertion. His method of dealing with the will to power of human beings was to invert it to a will to resist the despotism and tyranny of others. In a letter to the physician Benjamin Rush he wrote, "I have sworn upon the altar of God, eternal hostility against every form of tyranny over the mind of men" (Bartlett 1968, 472).

A universal moral sense or conscience was for Jefferson a basis of our common humanity and natural equality. It was what made persons capable of determining their own form of government by consent. This equality was for Jefferson universal and it included women, American Indians (Jefferson [1785] 1972, 227), and blacks (Jefferson [1785] 1972, 142). It was a matter of both self-affirmation and self-assertion, and this can help us understand his great concern for religious freedom, public education, and the injustice of slavery.

Slavery was the tragic flaw in the founding of American government. Jefferson was a slaveholder and this cannot be dismissed as only a concession to the society in which he lived. It was in his own self-interest and it allowed him to live an aristocratic lifestyle. He thus contributed to this tragedy. Yet, he understood the moral bankruptcy of slavery, its moral incompatibility with democratic government, and the need for its eventual abolition.

Jefferson felt that slavery could not be immediately abolished without the threat of great violence because of past injustices to blacks and the deeply held prejudices of whites. He had unsuccessfully recommended laws which would have achieved gradual but total emancipation, colonization of gradually emancipated slaves, and exclusion of slavery from all Western Territories (see also Jefferson [1785] 1972, 214). His diatribe against the king for allowing slavery to become established in the colonies was omitted from the final draft of the Declaration of Independence. At the time of the Missouri Compromise of 1820, he described the threat of the slavery issue to the Union as a "firebell in the night," and he wrote, "we have a wolf by the ears, and we can neither hold him, nor safely let him go. Justice is in the one scale, and self-preservation in the other" (Peterson 1977, 568). More than thirty years earlier he had written, "I tremble for my country when I reflect that God is just; that his justice cannot sleep forever..." (Jefferson [1785] 1972, 163).

Jefferson's proposal to abolish slavery after 1800 in all territories and future territories was defeated in committee by one vote. Concerning this he later commented: "Thus we see the fate of millions of unborn hanging on the tongue of one man, and heaven was silent in that awful moment" (Kenyon 1980). Jefferson understood the moral dimensions of freedom and he put them forth in stating the ideals of a new nation.

In practice, a civil war and several constitutional amendments were necessary to make universal equality as a principle and as the basis of the democratic process something of a reality. The issue over which there finally could be no compromise on slavery was the political assertion by John C. Calhoun and some in the southern states that slavery was not a moral wrong that had to be tolerated temporarily, but that it was a positive good.

Lincoln never wavered in his assertion that slavery was morally wrong and he opposed its extension into the territories. He also opposed resolving the issue of slavery in the territories, as Senator Douglas had proposed, by making it a matter of local popular sovereignty. Yet, he initially fought, and probably could not have otherwise won, the Civil War on the issue of popular sovereignty and majority rule in a democratic republic. To preserve the Union, Lincoln needed both public opinion and the slaveholding border states of Missouri, Kentucky, Maryland, and Delaware. Lincoln tried to uphold both the ideal in the Declaration of Independence of "a new nation, conceived in Liberty, and dedicated to the proposition that all men are created equal" and the rule of law in the Constitution of "government of the people, by the people, for the people."[8] Lincoln realized, however, that public opinion was needed to bring the ideals of universal equality into practice in a democratic republic.

VI
Conclusions, Current Reflections, and Summary
Conclusions

A secure future for our system of government does not require a different set of moral principles from those in the Declaration of Independence and our Constitution. Even great reformers, such as Martin Luther King, have simply asked that we put our original principles into practice. It is our difficulty in fully living up to our own ideals, individually and collectively, that has been referred to as the "promise of disharmony" (Huntington 1981). The future of constitutional democracy depends upon our continued efforts to reconcile our ideals and principles with the democratic process.

What was unique about James Madison and the Founding Fathers, however, was not just that they based government on the consent of the people, but that they based government on individuals and a people that they understood to be not always virtuous. The limitations and divisions, the checking of interest by interest, and the placing of constitutional law above the divisions of government were all directed toward placing restraints on both factions and majorities. Yet it was understood that in a pluralistic society the alternative to government by deliberation based on equality was government based on simple coercion or privilege. For this reason Madison understood the importance of the republican experiment that Jefferson called "the world's best hope" (Padover 1943, 385) and Lincoln called "the last, best hope of earth" (Basler 1953, vol. V, 537).

The United States Constitution was originally concerned primarily with freedoms from the potential abuses of governmental power. Since the Civil War, the dynamic political system created by that constitution, however, has responded to political change and public opinion to address enabling freedoms and other moral issues of equality. The political franchise has been expanded almost universally. Other issues have been the definition of legal equality, an equality of opportunity and education, and more recently some issues of social equality. The degree of economic inequality has also been in part addressed with such measures as the curtailing of the excesses of laissez faire capitalism, a progressive income tax, and the development of a social welfare state.

Reflective writers, such as George Orwell, have urged us to accept the political, economic, and moral responsibilities of freedom because they were aware of how easily freedom can be lost. That is, if we value freedom, then we should establish the conditions for freedom and its survival. The several aspects of universal equality do provide a moral context for freedom and pluralism. It is the moral assertion of the dignity and worth of each individual, and its translation into several aspects of political equality concerning the coercive powers of government, that makes the accommodation and preservation of a wide variety of attributes, abilities, and desires possible.

Alexis de Tocqueville understood correctly, however, that equality misunderstood can threaten freedom. Indeed, equality misunderstood can threaten virtue or any moral distinction. Neither unrestricted equality nor unrestricted freedom can, therefore, serve as the practical basis of a pluralistic political community. American constitutional democracy is an attempt to reconcile and integrate these several ideals and principles—not only the sometimes conflicting claims of freedom and equality, but also the several different aspects of equality based on the multi-faceted nature of human beings. Such an understanding of our governmental system leaves us with an indeterminate but dynamic politics.[9]

Concerning *values,* ethics does involve the making of distinctions concerning right and wrong, perceived truth and justice, the common good, and distinctions in individual character and virtue. Whenever a hierarchy of *persons* is used to justify coercive power, however, it is often coercive power that ends up sustaining the hierarchy. The colonial founders were concerned with such abuse of the coercive powers of government by self-appointed and hereditary elites of kings, priests, and nobles. Jefferson could hardly be described as a Hobbesian or a Calvinist but he wrote, "Mankind soon learn to make interested uses of every right and power which they possess, or may assume" (Jefferson [1785] 1972, 121). He also wrote that he knew of "no safe depository of the ultimate powers of society but the people themselves..." (Malone, vol. 6, 353). Lincoln said simply, "No man is good enough to govern another man without that other's consent" (Basler 1953, vol. II, 226).

United States constitutional democracy attempts to achieve accommodation and resolution of conflict in a pluralistic society, without arbitrary coercion or alienation. It attempts to do this by limiting and dividing the powers of government and recognizing several aspects of equality. It is also a means, however, of collectively achieving and securing a wide spectrum of goals and values. Self-government or the development and expression of the mature, responsible personality, in the context of community, can itself, for example, be considered a moral goal.

After devoting much of his life to a study of the history of freedom, Lord Acton, an eighteenth century English historian, concluded that "Power tends to corrupt and absolute power corrupts absolutely" (Bartlett 1968, 750). A corollary might be added to this concerning sovereignty and the coercive powers of government—a system of political equality rewards virtue and merit more readily than a personal political hierarchy recognizes moral issues of equality. The constitutional democracy of the United States protects individual differences in beliefs and opinions. Within limits the government both allows and makes distinctions concerning values, natural circumstances, social conditions, and behavior. Although we must acknowledge our shortcomings in history, it is very important to recognize and understand that United States constitutional democracy also affirms an *equality of persons*. That is its primary moral assertion.

Current Reflections

The international political tragedy of the twentieth century, a century which coined the word genocide, bears witness to the need for universal concepts of equality. The basic political problem remains a tendency to divide the world and society into "we" versus "they", the inability to morally recognize our common humanity. The alienation of our times would also tend to affirm the need for integration – the need to individually and politically integrate the composite nature of our own humanity as well as the several aspects of the world in which we live.[10] Singular theories that have based order and moral authority on *only* material needs, an aspect of social conscience, reason, or a metaphysical or religious concept, or *only* on the individual, the state, natural science, or ideology, have often led to disintegration and individual or communal tragedy. By focusing on even perhaps a particular truth, in a quest for certainty, they have too easily justified the use of coercive force or been the cause of alienation.

Nor is it easy to imagine a resolution of the problems of alienation in our own society if individual rights and freedoms are not also understood in a moral context and associated with responsibilities. Individual rights and freedoms need to be understood in the larger ethical contexts of moral duty and reciprocity, normative behavior and reversibility, communal

79

values and responsibilities, and a commitment to defend similar rights and freedoms for others.

Furthermore, it is difficult to imagine an adequate resolution of the global problems which have resulted from technology without a concept of universal equality and our common humanity. Several writers, perhaps the most prominent being Konrad Lorenz, have noted that our technical progress has far exceeded the parameters of our biological adaptive mechanisms and moral structures. Among the problems which threaten the future of all peoples are those of nuclear or biological warfare, genetic engineering and population control in a time of scarce resources and a threatened environment, and the level of totalitarianism and terrorism which technology has made possible.

Even from the view of evolutionary development, it can be argued that natural selection may not favor a species that is unable to control aggression with structured ethical systems. A more balanced evolutionary theory, a greater understanding of the nearly symbiotic nature of our own biology, and game theory have all recently emphasized the importance of cooperation as a factor of natural selection (Axelrod 1984; Thomas 1975; Dawkins 1989, chap. 12). Ethical structure and cooperation are significant elements in the fitness of natural selection, much as they are often factors for peace and tranquility in psychology, sociology, natural law theory, and religion.

Summary

An analytical framework for moral and political philosophy has been presented. This framework takes into account the composite and integral nature of human beings and the several ways that we relate to the world in which we live. It is only meant to be a scaffolding and, therefore, it is far from complete. It does, however, provide a basis for understanding the several different aspects of universal equality which provide the moral foundations of United States constitutional democracy. These different

aspects of universal equality are also derived historically in Western civilization from ethical and legal systems
which are a prescriptive or instructional type of knowledge
and faith.

The government of the United States is a constitutional
democracy. Only by referring to it as such, can we understand
the several aspects of its "central idea" of universal equality.
In our system of government, universal equality is a "higher
law" substantive principle concerning the dignity and worth of
all persons and it is also the basis of a procedural concept of
equality in the democratic process. The moral aspects of universal equality exclude the coercive powers of government
from certain parts of our lives and give accountability to the
divisions of government which make, adjudicate, and enforce
our laws. We certainly need to recognize the value of other cultures, of other metaphors for understanding the nature of
human beings and how we relate to the world in which we live,
and of other frameworks of analysis. It is within the several
aspects of universal equality, however, that all people can
both assert their individuality against tyranny and also affirm
their humanity.

By balancing the several aspects of universal equality, constitutional democracy in the United States achieves some
recognition and integration of the individual, social, and natural moral constraints within which we live. Our form of
government, however, is also a recognition that some of our
highest aspirations, strongest commitments, and deepest
faiths neither can nor should be coerced by government.

Notes

1. See "Memory and Truth" by Craig Dykstra (1987) for a discussion of the role of memory in these functions.

2. It is understood that these categories are very general and that a capacity such as social conscience relates to several sometimes conflicting ethical concerns of "society" such as family, community, nationality, and inclusive humanity.

3. Regarding our need to orientate ourselves in both space and time, see Mircea Eliade's works *The Sacred and the Profane* (1961) and *The Myth of the Eternal Return* (1974).

4. Madison hoped that the Bill of Rights "might acquire by degree the character of fundamental maxims of free government, and as they become incorporated into the national sentiment, counteract the impulses of interest and passion" (see Diamond 1979,71).

5. Jefferson appreciated and attempted to emphasize the difference between constitutional and legislative processes (Jefferson [1785] 1972, 120–129).

6. "The *Nicomachean Ethics* exhibits indecision between two accounts of *eudaimonia*—a comprehensive and an intellectualist account. According to the intellectualist account, stated in Book X Chap. 7, *eudaimonia* is realized in the activity of the most divine part of man, functioning in accordance with its proper excellence. This is the activity of theoretical contemplation. According to the comprehensive account (described as secondary at 1178a 9) *eudaimonia* essentially involves not just the activity of the theoretical intellect, but the full range of human life and action, in accordance with the broader excellences of moral virtue and practical wisdom. This view connects *eudaimonia* with the conception of human nature as composite, i.e. as involving the interaction of reason, emotion, perception, and action in an ensouled body" (Nagel 1972,252).

7. The transition in theory is from citizenship by birthright to citizenship by consent (see Schuck and Smith 1985, chap. 1). Each concept of citizenship by itself has inherent problems.

8. It is probably not just a coincidence that these quotes are from the first and last lines of the Gettysburg Address.

9. "In large measure, a political judgment is usually 'judicial' in quality; that is, for the most part it involves a judgment concerning conflicting claims, all of which possess a certain validity. As Aristotle shrewdly pointed out, there is no problem of political judgment when one claim alone is admitted to be valid and enthroned above all the rest. The result of this condition, however, is that the political association is replaced by a state of seige (*Politics* III, xiii, 1283a 21–1283b). But once the political association is defined as a compound of many diverse parts, and once it is allowed that these 'parts' will have different opinions, interests, and claims, the politicalness of the judgment will depend on a sensitivity to diversities. A political judgment, in other words, is 'true' when it is public, not public when it accords to some standard external to politics" (Wolin 1960, 63).

10. Shirley Letwin describes integration as part of the cultural characteristics of the gentleman in *The Gentlemen in Trollope: Individuality and Moral Conduct* (1983). Kenneth Minogue did an excellent review of this book (1983).

References

Axelrod, Robert. 1984. *The Evolution of Cooperation.* New York: Basic Books.

Barrett, William. 1986. *Death of the Soul.* Garden City, N.Y.: Anchor Press/Doubleday.

Bartlett, John. 1968. *Familiar Quotations,* fourteenth edition. Boston: Little, Brown

Basler, Roy P., ed., 1953. *The Collected Works of Abraham Lincoln,* vols. New Brunswick, N.J.: Rutgers University.

Calvin's Case. 1608. 7 Co. Rep. 15b.

Corwin, Edward S. 1955. *The "Higher Law" Background of American Constitutional Law.* Ithica, N.Y.: Cornell University.

Davis, David Brion. 1990. *Revolutions: Reflections on American Equality and Foreign Liberations.* Cambridge, Mass.: Harvard University.

Dawkins, Richard. 1989. *The Selfish Gene.* New York: Oxford University.

Diamond, Martin. 1979. "Ethics and Politics: The American Way." *In The Moral Foundations of the American Republic,* ed. Robert H. Horwitz. Charlottesville Va.: University of Virginia.

Dr. Bonham's Case. 1610. 8 Co. 118a.

Dykstra, Craig. 1987. "Memory and Truth." *Theology Today,* vol. XLIV, No. 2.

Eliade, Mircea, 1961. *The Sacred and the Profane.* New York: Harper and Brothers.

Eliade, Mircea. 1974. *The Myth of the Eternal Return.* Princeton, N.J.: Princeton University.

Foner, Phillip, ed., 1950. *Basic Writings of Thomas Jefferson.* Garden City, N.Y.: Halcyon House.

Forkosch, Morris D. 1973. "Due Process in Law." In *Dictionary of the History of Ideas,* ed. Phillip P. Wiener. New York: Charles Scribner's Sons.

Hamilton, Alexander, James Madison, and John Jay. [1787–88] 1961. *The Federalist Papers.* New York: New American Library.

Hill, Christopher. 1975. *The World Turned Upside Down.* Harmondsworth, Middlesex, England: Penguin Books.

Hobbes, Thomas [1651] 1981. *Leviathon,* ed. C.B. Macpherson. Harmondsworth, Middlesex, England: Penguin Books.

Huntington, Samuel P. 1981. *American Politics: The Promise of Disharmony.* Cambridge, Mass.: Harvard University.

Jaffa, Henry V. 1982 ed. *Crisis of the House Divided: An Interpretation of the Issues of the Lincoln-Douglas Debates.* Chicago: University of Chicago.

Jefferson, Thomas [1785] 1972. *Notes on the State of Virginia.* New York: W.W. Norton and Company.

Kenyon, Cecelia M. 1980. "Thomas Jefferson." In the *Encyclopaedia Britanica,* 15th Edition, 30 vol. Chicago: Encyclopaedia Britanica.

Koch, Adrienne. 1964. *Jefferson and Madison: The Great Collaboration.* New York: Oxford University Press.

Koch, Adrienne. 1943. *The Philosophy of Thomas Jefferson.* New York: Columbia University.

Kohlberg, Lawrence. 1981. *The Philosophy of Moral Development,* vol. I. San Francisco: Harper and Row.

Konner, Melvin. 1983. *The Tangled Wing: Biological Constraints on the Human Spirit.* New York: Harper Colophon.

Lakoff, Sanford A. 1964. *Equality in Political Philosophy.* Cambridge, Mass.: Harvard University.

Letwin, Shirley Robin. 1982. *The Gentleman in Trollope: Individuality and Moral Conduct.* Cambridge, Mass.: Harvard University.

Lovejoy, Arthur O. 1936. *The Great Chain of Being.* Cambridge, Mass.: Harvard University.

Malone, Dumas. 1981. *Jefferson and His Time,* 6 vol. Boston: Little, Brown.

Marbury v. Madison. 1803. I cranch 137.

McWilliams, Wilson Carey. 1979. On Equality as the Moral Foundation for Community." In *The Moral Foundations of The American Republic,* ed. Robert H. Horwitz. Charlottesville, Va.: University of Virginia.

Meyers, Marvin, ed., 1981. *The Mind of the Founder; Sources of the Political Thought of James Madison,* revised ed. Hanover, N.H.: Brandeis University.

Minogue, Kenneth. 1983. "The Culture of the Gentleman." *Public Interest* No. 71, Spring.

Nagel, Thomas. 1972. "Aristotle on Eudaimonia." *Phronesis* 17:252–59.

Padover, Saul K., ed., 1943. *The Complete Jefferson.* New York: Tudor Publishing.

Paine, Thomas. [1776] 1982. *Common Sense,* ed. Isaac Kramnick. Harmondsworth, Middlesex, England: Penguin Books.

Peterson, Merrill D., ed., 1977. *The Portable Thomas Jefferson.* New York: Penguin Books.

Pollack, Ervin H. 1979. *Jurisprudence: Principles and Applications.* Columbus, Oh.: Ohio State University.

Randall, John Herman. 1926. *The Making of the Modern Mind.* New York: Columbia University.

Rawls, John. 1971. *A Theory of Justice.* Cambridge, Mass.: Harvard University.

Roberts, Clayton, and David Roberts. 1980. *A History of England,* 2 vol. Englewood Cliffs, N.J.: Prentice-Hall.

Sabine, George H., and Thomas L. Thorson. 1973. *A History of Political Theory,* 4th ed. Hinsdale, Ill.: Dryden Press.

Sagan, Carl. 1978. *The Dragons of Eden: Speculations on the Evolutions of Human Intelligence.* New York: Ballantine Brooks.

Schuck, Peter H., and Rogers M. Smith. 1985. *Citizenship Without Consent: Illegal Aliens in the American Polity.* New Haven: Yale University.

Stevenson, Leslie. 1987. *Seven Theories of Human Nature.* New York: Oxford University.

Thomas, Lewis. 1975. *The Lives of a Cell.* New York: Bantam Books.

Weber, Max. [1921] 1964. *The Theory of Economic and Social Organization,* 1st Paperback edition, ed. Talcott Parsons. New York: Free Press.

Wills, Garry. 1979. *Inventing America: Jefferson's Declaration of Independence.* New York: Vintage Books.

Wolin, Sheldon S. 1960. *Politics and Vision.* Boston: Little, Brown

"An Ecological Organic Paradigm: A Framework of Analysis for Moral and Political Philosophy" was originally published in the *Journal of Consciousness Studies,* Volume 6 (1999): October, pp. 81–103 and is reprinted here with permission.

An Ecological Organic Paradigm:

A Framework of Analysis
for Moral and Political Philosophy

Abstract: A modern version of the classical Greek organic paradigm can be based on behavioral ecology, ecology being the study of the interrelationships between an organism and its environment. The ecological organic paradigm describes four general human mental functional capacities—appetite, social conscience, reason and an interpretive capacity—and associates them, in the context of evolutionary and psychological development, to four general categories of experience—primal individual needs, society, the natural world in which we live and metaphysics— with which we have to cope, adapt, and interrelate. The ecological organic paradigm is compatible with both natural and cultural evolution. The framework can accommodate both descriptive and normative concepts of human nature and it can accommodate both the individual and social dimensions of human knowledge and activity.

The framework gives some coherence to the ethical categories. The questions, What is obligatory?, What is good?, What is fitting?, and What is humane?, are included within the framework as valid moral questions. Deontological, normative, communitarian and individual human concerns are all recognized.

One way to understand the ecological organic paradigm (EOP) is to contrast it with the general state of philosophy in the last one hundred years, which might be compared to the story of the blind men describing an elephant; each perspective describes a particular part but none gives a coherent view of the elephant. The EOP suggests that we reconsider, in the context of behavioral ecology, a modern version of the organic paradigm as at least one useful framework for describing the "elephant."

The EOP is a framework of analysis that has the ability to bring a greater degree of coherence to discussions in moral and *political philosophy and to provide a basis for accommodation in a pluralistic society and world community.*

But in truth justice was, as it seems, something of this sort; however, not with respect to a man's minding his external business, but with respect to what is within... he arranges himself, becomes his own friend, and harmonizes the three parts, exactly like three notes in a harmonic scale, lowest, highest and middle. And if there are some other parts in between, he binds them together and becomes entirely one from many, moderate and harmonized. Then and only then, he acts... In all these actions he believes and names a just and fine action one that preserves and helps to produce this condition, and wisdom the knowledge that supervises the action...

Plato, *The Republic,* Book IV, 443c

I. Introduction

An organic framework of analysis is not a new or postmodern idea. It is a premodern idea. There have been several versions of an organic paradigm, but the concept generally refers to some application of a classical Greek understanding of human nature as a composite whole. The organic paradigm has often referred to a model of human nature as being a composite of physical, social, mental and spiritual dimensions. This understanding of human nature has sometimes been described as a metaphor because it has been perceived to be like, or to have a correlation with, various aspects of the world in which we live.

The organic model of human nature was eventually replaced in philosophy for at least four reasons. The primary reason was that the organic paradigm in its hierarchical Platonic form, as the tripartite soul, had been used to support similar hierarchical structures in the Church and the state. It had been used, for example, to support the rule of the king and the Pope. Second, metaphors suggesting organicism in society have also been avoided in our times in part because Hegel extended organicism to a metaphysical concept of *Volkgeist* that was subsequently used in part to support a totalitarian nationalism in Germany. Third, Darwin's description of evolutionary development was misappropriated by the hierarchical ideology of Social Darwinism. Fourth, some aspects of modernism and postmodernism have been reluctant to recognize any natural or metaphysical constraints on either individual (or social) will and power.

Why, then, should we reconsider a modern version of the organic paradigm? The primary insight on this is that in the last one hundred years the biological sciences and medicine have tended to use categories similar to those of the organic paradigm, but have not necessarily interpreted the several dimensions of human nature to be hierarchical or ideological. Current interpretation would emphasize more a system of checks and balances for health and well-being. Second, a new Darwinism, which is less hierarchical and recognizes both natural and cultural evolution, or co-evolution, gives us sufficient conceptual space to reconsider the role of nature and an ecological version of the organic paradigm. Third, a broad enough definition of our interpretive capacity and metaphysics, on the other hand, can be used to again bring integrative and metaphysical considerations back to an appropriate place in academic discussions of moral and political philosophy. Fourth, the ecological organic paradigm is a framework of analysis that at least has the capacity for affirmation, accommodation, moderation, adaptation and synthesis. It has the capacity to accommodate pluralism in our own society and in the global community.

A modern version of the organic paradigm will prove to be a very useful tool or framework of analysis for understanding the dynamics of moral and political philosophy. An ecological organic paradigm can also bring some coherence to moral and political philosophy and it should be reconsidered.

II. An Ecological Organic Paradigm (EOP)

A modern version of the organic paradigm can be based on behavioral ecology, ecology being the study of the inter-relationships between an organism and its environment.[1] To do this from the standpoint of behavior and cognition, the organic paradigm needs to coincide with our general levels of awareness or consciousness and be expressed in terms of our mental functional capacities. The modern ecological organic paradigm (EOP) being proposed thus will have the perspective of an ecology of cognition or an ecology of the mind or consciousness. It describes four general human mental functional capacities, in the context of evolutionary and psychological development, and loosely associates them to four general categories of experience with which we have to cope, adapt and interrelate.

The four functional cognitive capacities are described as appetite, social conscience, reason and an interpretive capacity. The dimensions of experience to which they each primarily, but not exclusively, interrelate are primal individual needs, society, the natural world in which we live and metaphysics. "Interpretation" and "metaphysics" are being used here as broad categories that represent integration, orientation, and narrative, concerning meaning and purpose, and they represent our need for a coherent self and world in which we live. They have to do not so much with the natural world in which we live and of which we are a part, but with our individual and collective place in that world. This framework of analysis of four functional cognitive capacities and their interrelationship to four general dimensions of experience will be referred to as the ecological organic paradigm.

The general framework of analysis that is being proposed is a modification of the work of Leslie Stevenson in *Seven Theories of Human Nature* (1987). In this work, Stevenson states that the best way to understand any philosophy or philosopher is to understand the assumptions being made concerning the nature of human beings, the nature of society, and the nature of the universe. Since the Copernican Revolution, however, assumptions about the nature of the universe have been increasingly divided into assumptions concerning the natural world in which we live and metaphysical assumptions about meaning and purpose that integrate our knowledge and create a narrative in space and time. One set of assumptions concerns the question *how*. The other set of assumptions concerns the question *why*. The ecological organic framework for understanding the dynamics of moral and political philosophy being proposed thus has four very general categories rather than the three described by Stevenson. These consider the assumptions concerning the individual, society, nature, and metaphysics. Our capacities of cognition that primarily relate to each of these categories are sequentially described as appetite, social conscience, logical reasoning, and an interpretive capacity for integration and narrative.

This modern ecological organic paradigm is derived in part from classical philosophy. It is also compatible, however, with some recent concepts that include both natural and cultural evolution (co-evolution) and some recent concepts of psychological cognitive development. This perspective not only includes both nature and nurture, but also sees an interrelationship between them. There is freedom within form. Human nature is neither seen to be infinitely malleable by changing its social context, nor is it seen as only determined by evolution and genetics. James Q. Wilson, in *The Moral Sense,* wrote that, "two errors arise in attempting to understand the human condition. One is to assume that culture is everything, the other is to assume that it is nothing" (1993, p. 6). At the human level, evolution in the broadest sense entails cultural history, but our cultural history in the broadest sense also entails evolution. Human history, in this perspective, did not begin 5000 years ago with the written word.

This framework can accommodate both descriptive and normative concepts of human nature, and it can accommodate both the individual and social dimensions of human knowledge and activity. In this framework moral and political philosophy are perceived to be dynamic, not only because human nature is multidimensional, but also because the experiences to which we relate change and are changeable. The different dimensions of our cognition, whether they be "gut reactions" or rational reflections, enable us to deal with both internal and external environmental complexity (Godfrey-Smith, 1996). Because of these multiple factors one does not anticipate a convergence through reductionism, such as one sometimes sees in the basic sciences (Flanagan, 1997).[2] Such reductionism has sometimes been referred to as physics envy. On the other hand, the logical implication of such a framework is not necessarily subjectivity, relativism, arbitrariness, or material utility, but more toward what Aristotle described as *phronesis* or practical wisdom. It should thus not be unexpected that the paradigm also is compatible with the categories of what is sometimes called a "folk psychology," which is based on introspection and accumulated experience. This framework of an ecological organic paradigm is not entirely new for it is based in part, for example, on Aristotle's sense of the composite whole and it addresses the problem of the one and the many. It is a reconsideration of an old and common idea.

The Classical Origins of the Organic Paradigm

The Greek philosophers not only understood man to be a political animal, that is meant to live in a *polis* or community, but also understood the community to reflect the parts of human nature as a body politic (Hale, 1973). This type of inquiry by analogy is the method of reasoning used in Plato's *Republic*. The organic metaphor of the "body politic" is a source in Western civilization of such important political concepts as mixed government, the division of power by function and the separation of church and state. For the Greek philosophers *eudaimonia* (translated as meaning and purpose or happiness) for the individual was analogous to what lead to the highest good or *summum bonum* for the state. Political philosophy was an extension of moral philosophy and *eudaimonia* was not something apart from goodness and virtue. Plato compared the concerns and skills of an ideal ruler to the concerns and skills of a physician treating a patient.

As Aristotle noted, there is an intrinsic and teleological element in the unity, order, and wholeness of living organisms which confers appropriate function or "purpose" on the multiplicity of their parts. The acorn, to use Aristotle's example, given the proper conditions, has the potential or inherent design to become an oak. In his aesthetic theory, Immanuel

94

Kant drew an analogy between the organic units of a work of art and a living body. He also, however, made distinctions. In a living organism the "parts produce one another: it is self-organizing"; an organism that goes out of order "repairs itself"; and a natural organism can reproduce itself (Orsini, 1973). This is a recognition that living organisms have an intrinsic order to develop, sustain and reproduce life. This is sometimes described as an immanent teleology as opposed to a cosmic teleology (Arnhart, 1988; Lennox, 1993).

Thomas Nagel in "Aristotle and *Eudaimonia*" (1972, p. 252) wrote that:

> "The Nichomachean Ethics exhibits indecision between two accounts of *eudaimonia*—a comprehensive and an intellectualist account. According to the intellectualist account, stated in Book X Chap. 7, *eudaimonia* is realized in the activity of the most divine part of man, functioning in accordance with its proper excellence. This is the activity of theoretical contemplation. According to the comprehensive account (described as secondary at 1178a 9) *eudaimonia* essentially involves not just the activity of the theoretical intellect, but the full range of human life and action, in accordance with the broader excellences of moral virtue and practical wisdom. This view connects *eudaimonia* with the conception of human nature as composite, i.e. as involving the interaction of reason, emotion, perception, and action in an ensouled body."

From a different perspective, Aristotle understood a human being or man to be an animal, a "political animal," a rational animal, and a contemplative animal that pursues *eudaimonia*.

It is the recognition of the multiple dimensions of human nature that will be the most productive part of an ecological organic framework. The great synthesizers of thought in Western civilization, such as Plato, Aristotle, St. Thomas Aquinas and Kant, utilized the multiple aspects of human nature in their systematic constructs. A similar organic functional approach, in an ecological context, can be useful for an analytical framework of analysis.

The ecological organic paradigm being described attempts to give a useful description of the dynamic aspects of human nature from the standpoint of our mental functional capacities and their interrelationship with internal and external environmental complexity. It is meant to be a general framework of analysis without necessarily subscribing to a particular ideology. As a metaphor, there is no claim of exclusivity. There are more reductive metaphors, such as Cartesian dualism, and there are more expansive metaphors, such as "the fabric of life." A metaphor that has its origins in classical philosophy and has similar components to those of an ecological organic framework is the ship metaphor as described by C. S. Lewis (1943, p. 70–71). A successful expedition requires that each ship be in order and seaworthy, that the ships be able to sail together as a fleet without running into one another or getting separated and lost, that there is the knowledge and skill to successfully navigate to the destination, and that there is a purpose fulfilled by going to the destination or making the journey. Without claiming exclusivity, the ecological organic paradigm is meant to be a generalized framework of analysis that can be used to bring some coherence to understanding a similar dynamics in moral and political philosophy.

The Organic Paradigm in Folk Psychology

Paul Churchland, one of the leading philosophers of neurobiology, recently wrote in *The Engine of Reason, The Seat of the Soul* (1995) of the persistence of our conceptual commitments to the general categories of "folk psychology," which are similar to those of the ecological organic paradigm. Churchland thinks that the developing understanding of neurological mechanisms and artificial intelligence will change our common ideas about cognition and consciousness. He thus makes what he describes as an uncertain challenge to "our shared portrait of ourselves as self-conscious creatures with beliefs, desires, emotions, and the power of reason." He states that

> "this conceptual frame is the unquestioned possession of every normal human who wasn't raised from birth by wolves.

96

It is the template of our normal socialization as children; it is the primary vehicle of our social and psychological commerce as adults; and it forms the background matrix for our current moral and legal discussions. It is often called "folk psychology" by philosophers, not as a term of derision, but to acknowledge it as a basic descriptive and explanatory conceptual framework with which all of us currently comprehend the behavior and mental life of our fellow humans and ourselves" (pp. 18–19).[3]

There does not need to be a dichotomy, however, between the physiological mechanisms described by Churchland and the functional categories described in folk psychology and an ecological organic paradigm.

Churchland describes various types of learning as the development of prototypes through experience. These prototypes develop a physiological and anatomical basis. Concerning our visual capacity, for example, there are mechanisms in our visual neural network that develop and allow us to more readily perceive a straight line. By a mechanism of vector processing and completion we can learn to visually perceive a straight line by pattern recognition, inference, and even illusion. It is interesting to note that the concept of a straight line, which is one of the axioms of Euclidean geometry accepted by definition rather than proof, has a basis in our visual mechanism once it is developed from natural experience. This natural capacity for visual development that is molded by experience, like our capacity to learn language, can be subverted by sensory deprivation. Euclidian geometry considers the few axioms from which it is derived to be self-evident. The ability to recognize a straight line is at least adaptive for our survival. It is important for such things as maintaining a vertical posture and recognizing predators and prey. This does not, however, preclude non-Euclidian geometries. Explanations in evolutionary epistemology are often perceived to be adaptive to the environment by natural selection.

Jefferson believed that we have a natural capacity for a "moral sense" arguing that, since we were made to live in society, "He who made us would have been a pitiful bungler if he had made us without an inherent capacity to do so" (Peterson 1977, p. 424). Jefferson saw our capacity for a moral sense, however, as a potential that needed to be developed by use as does the strength of a muscle. He noted that there may also be defects as with other attributes. Jefferson considered the capacity for a moral sense to be common to all humanity, including American Indians and blacks (Jefferson, 1785/1972, p. 142, p. 227). He also wrote that, if you state a moral question to a ploughman and a professor, the former will decide it as well, and often better than the latter, because he has not been lead astray by artificial rules (Peterson 1977, p. 424).

A current example of folk psychology can be found in the enormously successful self-help book by Steven R. Covey, *The 7 Habits of Highly Effective People* (1989, p. 288). In a chapter entitled "Sharpening the Saw", he addresses the need to improve our physical, social, mental, and spiritual capacities. Covey also describes instances in which we may have a "mini-paradigm" shift and re-see the moral salience of a situation. Peggy DesAutels, in an essay entitled "Gestalt Shifts in Moral Perception", uses an example from Covey's book to describe how we can shift within our conceptual categories and within our learned, diverse, moral prototypes (as described by Churchland) to adjust to a changing context (1997, pp. 129–143). Covey's book can also be useful in describing the benefits of our capacity for intentionality and purpose. The first two habits of highly effective people are to begin with the end in mind and to be proactive.

If one considers any group of friends, some will usually be recognizable as functioning primarily in a physical, social, rational, or interpretive mode of being, though we all incorporate each of these elements in our personality.

The Organic Paradigm in Evolutionary and Psychological Development

A theory of the progressive evolutionary development of the brain, which can be extended to support the cognitive categories of the ecological organic paradigm, is Paul MacLean's concept of the *triune brain* (Sagan 1977, pp. 57–83; Konner 1983, pp. 147–152; Adams and Victor 1993, pp. 411–12). The triune brain model describes the progressive evolutionary development of three layers of the forebrain which MacLean believes can still be distinguished neuroanatomically and functionally in our own brain structure. He describes initially a "reptilian complex" which surrounds the midbrain and which probably evolved several million years ago. It relates to such primal instincts as sex, survival, and aggression. This is surrounded by a limbic system that is fully developed in mammals, but not in reptiles. He relates the limbic system primarily to emotions and a social capacity other than primal hierarchy. Surrounding the rest of the brain is the neocortex, which in humans makes up by far the largest portion of the brain and is associated with reason. One could add to this, at least functionally, the language centers in the left hemisphere of the brain, which enhance our capacities for the abstract thinking, memory, and imagination needed for integration and narrative. Ludwig Wittgenstein, for example, when speculating on the extent to which ideas may be independent of the language used to express them, wrote, "The limits of my language mean the limit of my world" (1922, 5.6). Sir John Eccles, in *Evolution of the Brain: Creation of the Mind* (1989), noted that the human brain shows special enlargement in the frontal lobe associated with planning, projecting the future, and perhaps abstract thought and in the language areas of the left hemisphere. He refers to these areas as the neo-neocortex.

The functions of the human brain are dynamic and integrated. They have what has been described as "cognitive fluidity" (Mithen, 1996, Chapter 11). From the perspectives of both evolution and developmental psychology, however, the four categories are broadly descriptive of our mental development.

In the field of child developmental psychology, Jean Piaget described the progressive development of our mental capacities. The work of Lawrence Kohlberg in *The Philosophy of*

Moral Development: Moral Stages in the Idea of Justice (1981) is an extended application of the work of Piaget. Kohlberg's central premise is that our moral development is not unlike the development of our other mental behavior. He describes a mental and moral development in the child that begins with concrete self-oriented reasoning and progresses to social reasoning, then logical reasoning, and finally abstract reasoning (see also, however, Flanagan 1991, pp. 119–173; Gilligan 1982; and Lapsley 1992). An argument can be made that our individual mental and moral development recapitulates the evolutionary development of our mental capacities. It is interesting that, in a somewhat similar manner, F. M. Cornford in *Before and After Socrates* (1932) described classical Greek civilization as progressing from the *concrete* thought of Homer, to the *social* thought of Athens in the time of Pericles, to the *logical scientific reasoning* of the pre-Socratics, Hippocrates, and Thucydides, and culminating in the more *abstract* thought of the classical philosophers (see also Finley, 1966).

Some Qualification of the Cognitive Capacities

The basic assumption of the ecological organic paradigm is that the four described cognitive capacities or mental functions were advantageous and adaptive coping mechanisms in natural and cultural evolution.[4] The four cognitive categories are very general and inclusive and are intentionally described as capacities or potentials. Because of their derivation in evolutionary development as capacities and their similar progressive appearance in individual psychological development related to experience, these cognitive categories are expected to have some universal applicability as a framework of analysis. The interpretive capacity is integrative and it is thus not radically separated from practical perception and action, feelings, or empirical thought. All of the categories are perceived to be interactive and dynamic. The ecological interrelationships described are only primary and not exclusive.

Our many social interrelationships extending from our family to our common humanity, for example, are related to a

100

diverse array of social capacities which have broadly and collectively *for the purpose of analysis* been described as our social conscience. Our social interactions, however, are also obviously affected in a dynamic way by our other attributes of appetite, reason, and interpretation. Charles Darwin wrote that "ultimately our moral sense or conscience becomes a highly complex sentiment—originating in the social instincts, largely guided by the approbation of our fellow-man, ruled by reason, self-interest, and in later times by deep religious feelings, and confirmed by instruction and habit" (1936, p. 500).

The cognitive function described as "interpretation", which is being correlated with metaphysics, is to be understood as a broad category.[5] It refers to our ability to integrate the various dimensions of our life into a whole and our ability to orient ourselves in time and space through narrative. As a category of analysis, it is meant to accommodate both religious concepts of the soul and secular concepts of the self. The term "metaphysics" is also being used in a broad way as a general category. It is not being specified as either simply an order that we project upon the world or simply a natural order of the world that we perceive, intuit, or has been revealed to us. This also is probably not an either/or issue (Penrose 1994, p. 414; Lachterman 1989; Barrett 1986, part II). As a general framework of analysis the categories are meant to be inclusive.

Broadly defined, the cognitive capacity for metaphysical interpretation is not only a part of human nature, but it may be the most distinguishing part of human nature (Mayr 1988, p. 75).[6,7] Like our other cognitive capacities of appetite, social conscience and logical reasoning, our cognitive capacity for interpretation can be seen as an adaptive mechanism of selective advantage. In his book *An Anthropologist from Mars; Seven Paradoxical Tales,* Oliver Sacks suggests, "a new view of the brain, a sense of it not as programmed and static, but rather as dynamic and active . . . ceaselessly adapting to all the needs of the organism—its need above all, to construct a coherent self and world" (1995, p. xvii). The dynamics of this could be described better, however, by using the phrase "to construct and understand" a coherent self and world.

The cognitive capacity of appetite is similar to the "appetite" described by Plato, the "reptilian complex" described by MacLean, and the id described by Freud. It represents the self-interested primal needs of the individual for such things as food, survival, and reproduction. Freud represented the id, it may be noted, as having little regard for problems of self-contradiction or coherence.

It is also understood that most societies, from an anthropological perspective, have not markedly distinguished scientific from metaphysical concepts of the universe. Freud, in his psychological framework of analysis, had only three categories because he combined logical, empirical reasoning (that reasoning related to the reality principle) and interpretive, integrative reasoning together within the category of ego. The ecological organic framework, nevertheless, remains very useful for it can also clarify such points.

III. A Framework of Analysis for Understanding the Dynamics of Moral and Political Philosophy

An underlying premise of the modern ecological organic paradigm is that with the combination of natural and cultural evolution there is an interaction between an organism and its environment. Human beings are not perceived to be just a passive mirror of nature though we are a part of nature. One could argue from several perspectives for the fitness of the planet Earth toward the development of life, and also for the tremendous adaptive advantages of any kind of intelligence or cooperation for natural selection (Henderson 1970; Axelrod 1984). One could also argue that the external natural world in which we live is indifferent to our particular fate. One could also hold both positions. Another of the premises of the organic paradigm, however, is that, at least by natural selection through evolution, we are not indifferent to our fate. Being proactive and goal oriented has been an evolutionary advantage and it has been "highly effective." As living organisms that evolved through a process of natural selection, we have basic instincts for survival, food, and reproduction. The long dependency of our childhood requires social abilities and we have the capacity for reason. We have intentionality. We have a capacity to transcend our environment and, to a limited but significant degree, choose alternative futures. *If* one postulates the goals of human prosperity and posterity, *then* moral and political values become conditional factors for achieving these ends. Right reason is not the same as objective scientific reason. Natural Law is not the same as the law of nature (Corwin 1955). Natural Law is not just descriptive, but normative and prescriptive.

A first premise that can help define a moral system is that moral behavior is distinguished by an *affirmation* of life, even though this does not always mean preserving life at all costs. This premise refers, in general, to an affirmation of life that both attempts to overcome adversity and aspires to flourish. This quality of moral concerns has been described as "depth" and it distinguishes morality from a "value neutral" ethics (Kekes 1989). "Depth" relates to a distinction of values that affirms life and contributes to our well-being.

A second premise that can help define a moral system is the issue of inclusion or what has been described as "breadth" (Kekes 1989). From the models that help define an ecological organic paradigm, it can be concluded that for a moral system to be what has been described as sufficiently "broad," it needs to be inclusive of each of the multiple dimensions of human nature and perspectives of the world in which we live.

Much of our discourse could be clarified by recognizing both "breadth" and "depth" in moral philosophy. There are, for example, two great moral traditions in Western civilization.[8] The first is from classical civilization and is based primarily on a distinction of values regarding such things as truth, goodness, and beauty and such qualities as virtue. The second concerns the equal dignity and worth of individuals as persons and is derived primarily from Judeo-Christian sources

103

such as the Golden Rule and imago Dei and later Kant's categorical imperative. The concept of moral "depth", refers to an affirmation of life and *a distinction of values that relates primarily to attributes and behavior.* The concept of moral "breadth" extends this affirmation to the individual, the social community, our common humanity, concerns about the natural world in which we live, and metaphysical concepts of meaning and purpose. For a moral system to have sufficient "breadth," for example, there needs to be a *respect for persons and an affirmation of our common humanity.* The two ethical systems are often confused in dialogue when there is no recognition of the difference between an *equality of persons* and a *distinction of values that relates to attributes and behavior.*

In summary, by these definitions of a dimensional moral system of "breadth" and "depth" there are valid moral concerns *if* we affirm our individual selves, a premise of community, our common humanity, and a concept of causation and intergenerational continuity. In addition, there needs to be an acknowledgment of some of the natural possibilities and constraints within which we live. Without making such distinctions and definitions moral discourse, in general, becomes very confused and ambiguous. Morality would thus be defined as having at least some parameters within the larger field of ethical discourse and inquiry.[9]

The organic paradigm is compatible with an affirmation of life as the basis of a distinction of values or "depth." It is also able to accommodate "breadth", which extends the affirmation of our individual dignity and worth to our common humanity. It provides some coherence, for example, for the ethical and meta-ethical categories. It provides a basis for accommodation or what John Rawls has referred to as an overlapping consensus (1993; see also Lippman 1955, chap. 11 and Minogue 1983). The questions *What is obligatory?, What is good?, What is fitting?, and What is humane?* are all included within the organic framework as valid moral questions. Deontological, normative, communitarian, and individual human concerns are all recognized. Recognizing the dynamic

104

aspects of human nature and the world in which we live will not satisfy those in a quest for certainty, but it will be very valuable as a tool and framework of analysis.

A multidimensional understanding of human nature and the complex environment in which we live, results in the recognition of multiple ends and goals. It is important, therefore, that the procedure for choosing between such competing and sometimes conflicting goals attempts to do justice to the ends. The means need to do justice to the ends. In our individual lives this often involves the issue of integrity. "Integrity" has the same origin as the word "integer" and it refers to wholeness.

Shirley Letwin described integration as part of the cultural characteristics of the gentleman in *The Gentleman in Trollope; Individuality and Moral Conduct* (1982). The term "gentleman" was for her not gender specific. The gentleman is marked off by a conception of his own integrity and a concern for the coherence of his own life, thoughts and actions. He moves through life "constantly repairing the tears and gaps in the fabric of life caused by passion and misfortune" (Minogue, 1983). This can be contrasted with a more dialectical Freudian view of the self-divided man perceived as being in conflict with himself. As a framework of analysis, the EOP can recognize both the possibilities and the limitations of these views of human nature.

In a broader context, the ecological organic framework of analysis suggests that one could analyze and compare political philosophers or philosophies by placing them on a graph. One axis would represent a spectrum that would extend from the individual to society. The other axis would extend from science or materialism to metaphysics or idealism. One could also add a third vertical axis that would represent the degrees of coercive power in the system.

There has been some reluctance in legal theory to consider an organic framework of analysis as this doesn't always lead to a clearly preferable answer, let alone one right answer, in the very difficult cases. As a framework of analysis, the EOP would correctly be perceived to be an umbrella term that can incorporate diverse tendencies in moral and political philosophy. At the bottom of our legal system we rely on the procedure of a vote by a jury to determine the facts in a case. At the top of our judicial system we rely on the procedural vote of nine Supreme Court Justices to interpret the laws, which are sometimes conflicting. Yet, in explaining how the judges themselves decide these very difficult cases, Benjamin Cardozo in *The Nature of the Judicial Process* (1921) resorted to something very close to folk psychology or common sense philosophy. He wrote, "I can only answer that he must get his knowledge . . . from experience and study and reflection; in brief from life itself" (113; see also, Breyer 1998).

Political philosophy and government by definition involve community, and government also concerns the use of coercive power. Government, in one view, can be considered a monopoly of coercive power (Weber 1921/1964, p. 154). It arises in part, as Hobbes pointed out, from the need to avoid anarchy. Rousseau noted, however, that even the strongest are not strong enough to rule without converting obedience into a sense of duty. It is the *self-imposed moral foundations* of government that change mere obedience to the coercive powers of government into a sense of consensual responsibility for a moral duty, a just order, the common good, and human rights.

The modern organic framework that has been described can be used for the purposes of general political analysis. The ecological organic paradigm can also be used to analyze considerations of "breadth" and "depth" in moral philosophy. The framework of analysis considers the assumptions concerning the individual, society, nature, and metaphysics. It incorporates what we may understand and do, based on our cognitive capacities of appetite, social conscience, reason and interpretation.

IV. Why the Organic Paradigm was Abandoned in Philosophy and Why it should be Reconsidered

The organic framework in its hierarchical Platonic form, along with such other metaphors as The Great Chain of Being, was used primarily to support the prevailing social structures and institutions of the times. For 1500 years such metaphors helped to provide support for the hierarchy in the Church and the state. King James I of England understood the importance and spectrum of such paradigms of thought when he was reported to have said "No bishop, no king" (Roberts and Roberts 1980, p. 328).

The Scientific Revolution challenged the assumptions of the past and the Renaissance and the Reformation placed increased emphasis on the dignity and worth of each individual. The organic paradigm was thus eventually replaced in moral and political philosophy primarily by the concept of the social contract, which begins with the premise that all persons are born free and equal in a state of nature. The Stoic concept of equality, that we all have sufficient reason to understand a natural moral order, was always burdened in its challenge to hierarchy because the populace was illiterate and because in the Platonic framework of human nature reason was also used to justify hierarchy. The hierarchical social structures were more successfully challenged by Judeo-Christian concepts of equality based on ethical monotheism and love of one another with the best examples occurring when the particular religious beliefs were in a minority position. Moral and political concepts of equality, however, have been most widely accepted when they have been based on a concept of human rights that can be understood at the level of self-interest.

Moral theory also became more secular in what came to be widely perceived as a mathematical and mechanical universe. This view of an orderly world was also often accommodated and appropriated by a more natural theology. Such changes, it was thought, might also make possible a utilitarian determination of human well-being, not by seeking such uncertain principles as truth, goodness, beauty, and virtue, but by an egalitarian calculation of the consequence of actions in the terms of pleasure and pain.

Currently there are several reasons, however, why an organic paradigm should be reconsidered.

1. Developments in the biological sciences and medicine in the past one hundred years would tend to place a greater emphasis on a more balanced concept of human nature. Current scientific thought now considers feedback mechanisms and a system of checks and balances to be almost an essential part of the definition of a living organism. One example of a more balanced concept would be what Claude Bernard called the "internal milieu." This is the metabolic homeostasis of the internal environment or extracellular fluid in which our cells all live and which they monitor and help to maintain. Another example from medicine would be a current model used to evaluate pain (American Medical Association 1993, p. 307).

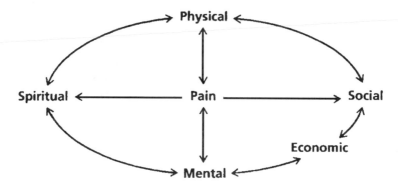

The basis of even a utilitarian calculation of the greatest good, based on pleasure and pain, can thus be seen to depend on the categories of the older organic paradigm and folk psychology. These categories are compatible with those of a modern ecological organic paradigm and the framework need not necessarily be hierarchical.

2. As will be shown in an extended example to follow, the framework of analysis of the organic metaphor is even instrumental to a historical and analytical understanding of the social contract, the primary paradigm that replaced it. The general categories of the organic framework, but not their earlier hierarchical form, are instrumental to an understanding of

the several aspects of equality on which United States constitutional democracy, as a social contract, is founded.

3. A central problematic or political issue of our time is the accommodation of pluralism. The ecological organic paradigm recognizes the multiple dimensions of human nature and, therefore, does not aspire to certainty or necessarily support any singular ideology. It does, however, provide a framework that at least has a capacity for accommodating pluralism. Recognizing, even very broadly, the multiple potentials of human nature can provide a rational basis for at least a threshold of values and conditions for the realization of those potentials as well as a basis for moderation and balance.

4. A barrier to learning in the past has often been the unavailability of information. A barrier to learning in the near future will be the difficulty of both selecting from an overabundance of information and associating such information in a meaningful way. A modern organic paradigm should be reconsidered because it can provide a useful framework for understanding the dynamics of moral and political philosophy. Folk psychology, as an equivalent of the ecological organic paradigm, has survived because it has provided some coherence. The ecological organic paradigm does not attempt to describe the specific anatomical mechanisms of perception and cognition. It provides coherence because it describes, in a general way, those cognitive functions that have progressively developed as coping mechanisms in both natural and cultural evolution.

5. A new Darwinism, which recognizes both natural and cultural evolution, rejects the false exclusionary dichotomies of nature versus nurture, fact versus value, and nature versus free will (Arnhart, 1995). If facts are not related to values, for example, the phrase "political science" is an oxymoron. In practice our perception of the facts usually has a very significant influence on our moral and political decisions. A more accurate description of the relationship would be that what we perceive to be the facts is not the *sole* determinant of our values. By recognizing the multiple dimensions of human nature, the ecological organic framework is able to

accommodate what were previously sometimes seen as either/or dichotomies.

6. As a metaphor, the ecological organic paradigm will remind us of the interrelationship between the character of the people and the character of the state. In his First Inaugural Address (Allen, 1988, p. 462), George Washington stated that it was imperative "that the foundations of national policy be laid in the pure and inimitable principles of private morality." Aristotle, on the other hand, understood the central role of the polis or community in forming individual character. Our individual and social moral character has perhaps become the most significant factor in the survival of ourselves, our society, our environment, and intergenerational continuity.

7. Ecology changes. We live in a nuclear age that has seen defense strategies of mutual assured destruction and response times measured in minutes. We will be facing the moral problems of genetic engineering and population control under the conditions of limited resources and a threatened environment. Technology has markedly increased the possibilities of both totalitarianism and terrorism. Yet we live in a century that coined the word "genocide" and a century that will be identified with individual alienation. The general concern has been that our technological development may have exceeded the parameters of our biological adaptive mechanisms and our moral development. We also live in a time of pluralism in our own culture and in what is increasingly becoming a pluralistic global community. As the sociologist Max Weber described, this degree of pluralism usually requires societies to be based on legal authority, rather than traditional kinship-descent or charismatic social organization (Weber 1921/1964, p. 328). These conditions point to the need for moral and political structures that both affirm life and can accommodate pluralism. They illustrate the need for limitations and moderation, but also the need for a model with a capacity for synthesis. A modern version of the organic paradigm should be reconsidered because it can provide a framework that has the capacity for affirmation, accom-

modation, moderation, adaptation, coherence, and synthesis.

8. The recurrent interest in a naturalized epistemology perhaps began in 1969 with a paper by W. V. Quine, "Epistemology Naturalized", in which he wrote that, "epistemology goes on, though in a new setting and a clarified status. Epistemology, or something like it, simply falls into place as a chapter of psychology and hence of natural science" (1969/1996, p. 82). Psychology, however, is related to and needs to be understood in the context of the other biological sciences as well as the humanities and from the perspective of behavioral ecology. Toward the end of the *Origin of Species* Darwin wrote, "In the distant future I see open fields for far more important researches. Psychology will be based on the foundation . . . of the necessary acquirement of each mental power and capacity by gradation" (1936, p. 373). Our cognitive capacities, our consciousness and ability to know, have in the past developed and continue to develop as part of an interaction with the complex world in which we live. The ecological organic paradigm can help to clarify the primary assumptions on which our thoughts and actions are based and take into consideration the contexts in which they occur.

9. In an article entitled "The Foundationalism in Irrealism, and the Immorality", the philosopher John F. Post (1996) states that "philosophers have tended to develop an image of themselves and their enterprise as largely independent of whatever the sciences might turn up." He quotes Wittgenstein as saying, "Darwin's theory has no more to do with philosophy than any other hypothesis in natural science" (Wittgenstein 1922, 4.1122). Post then writes, "But what happens when we consider concepts, language, and meaning not from the point of view of how they seem to us on reflection from within, but from the point of view of how they appear from without, in particular to biological science? By biological science I do *not* mean any of its possibly reductive subdisciplines, such as molecular biology or neuroscience, and certainly not any sociobiology. I mean the nonreductive, holistic biology of historically evolved living organisms in relation to their normal environments and to each

other." He continues that "One of the key notions of such biology is that of the *proper function* of an organ, device or behavior. For example, the proper function of the heart is to pump blood; to be a heart is to pump blood. Why?" He then sites Ruth Millikan in stating that the proper function of your heart is to pump blood because it was by pumping blood that past hearts (or enough of them) enabled containing organisms to survive and reproduce at rates higher than those without them. Post objects to language-game irrealism because it means that we who play the game are in charge only because of the rejection of relevant external constraints (Post, 1996, pp. 7–8).

The ecological organic paradigm takes the concept of "selection" seriously, but at the human level applies this both ways in the interaction between humans and their environment. The framework is based in the biological sciences, but it also retains a place for interpretation and metaphysics broadly understood.

V. Examples of the Ecological Organic Paradigm as a Framework of Analysis

Two examples will be used to illustrate the usefulness of the ecological organic framework of analysis in moral and political philosophy. The first will be an analytical and historical consideration of *equality,* which Jefferson[10], Madison[11], Tocqueville[12], and Lincoln[13] all considered the primary moral concept of United States constitutional democracy. For Jefferson the concept that "all men are created equal" was a moral assertion. This assertion is the first premise of the Declaration of Independence, which is argued in the manner of Euclidean geometry. It thus puts everything that follows, including life, liberty and the pursuit of happiness, into a moral context. For Jefferson the phrase was an affirmation of his own and our common humanity and it could thus be called a self-evident truth. The second example will use the ecological organic analytical framework to consider the several dimensions of the contemporary moral and political issue of abortion from the perspective of the physician.

Equality

The ecological organic framework of analysis helps to clarify the several different dimensions of the moral and political concept of universal equality. Within Western civilization there developed several sources of moral authority for law and several corresponding ethical and legal systems. Canon Law, Roman Law, English common law, and the social contract theory associated with constitutional law, each had a different primary source of moral authority. Each of these systems of law was, consequently, based on a different type of ethical system, and each focused primarily on a different facet of human nature. Constitutional democracy integrates aspects of these four ethical and legal systems as they relate to universal equality and the coercive powers of government.

Metaphysics and Interpretation: Canon Law, for example, was based on the authority of God and related primarily to what it understood to be the soul of man. Its ethic is deontological, deon meaning "duty" in Greek. That is, it is based on a universal duty "to love God with all thy heart, and with all thy soul, and with all thy strength, and with all thy mind; and thy neighbor as thyself" (Leviticus 19:18, Deuteronomy 6:5, Luke 10:27, Mark 12:29–31). This also happens to be an example of a use of the organic framework in a Judeo-Christian context. Canon Law contains universal ethical principles based on a reverence for God and reciprocity towards one's fellow man. The equal dignity and worth of all persons in this religious system derives from a belief in God and that man and woman were made in God's image (Gen 1:27). Equality is intrinsic and not derived from one's individual attributes, but from the relationship between God and humanity.

Nature and Reason: Roman Law, on the other hand, incorporated significant aspects of natural law based on the authority of a perceived natural moral order in the universe. Such a natural moral order could be understood by all persons, it was believed, because all humans share a capacity for right reason, an ability to know right from wrong. All of the various people within the vast Roman Empire, for example, could be expected to learn and know that it is wrong to steal. This ethical system of natural law is primarily normative (based on norms or ideals). Universal equality in classical civilization is based on all human beings having a capacity for right reason and also on a concept of reversibility (a reversal of position or fortune) which requires a rational imagination. Aristotle, in his *Poetics,* described reversibility as one of two major elements in Greek tragedies. The second element is catharsis, part of which is a realization that we all, even heroes and kings, have character flaws and are also subject to fate, both of which can lead to a reversal of fortunes. The more recent concept of justice as fairness as described by John Rawls in *The Theory of Justice* (1971), with an original position in which one does not know either his or her fate or circumstances in life's game, is an extension of the concept of reversibility.

Society and Social Conscience: Common law in English feudal society derived its moral authority from yet another source— not from God or nature, but from social custom and tradition. This was primarily a communitarian ethical system. It related to the social conscience of the people based on their concepts of rights and responsibilities in society. Traditional English rights progressively became a basis of communal solidarity.

The Individual and Appetite: Finally, the social contract theory associated with constitutional law derives its moral authority beginning with the individual in a state of nature concerned primarily about his own safety and happiness. Its very premise is not only that all are free and equal in a state of nature, but that everyone is also endowed with natural rights that they are entitled to defend. Such a theory is based on individual concerns and contract. The universality of social contract theory as it applies to democratic processes and constitutional law, however, makes it also essentially a humanitarian ethic. It contains an ethic of universal equality based on what we now refer to as human rights and a just claim to resist the violation of those rights.

American constitutional democracy integrates and balances

these four ethical perspectives as they apply to the several aspects of universal equality and the coercive powers of government. The accommodating common moral concept is not just a deontological ethic, with concepts of reverence and reciprocity, relating to God and a person's soul; nor is it just a normative ethic, based on concepts of right reason and reversibility, relating to a perceived moral order in nature and our capacity to understand that order with our reason; nor is it just a communitarian ethic, with concepts of social rights and responsibilities, as they relate to the several aspects of society and our social conscience; nor is it only an individual ethic, with a concept of human rights and the right to resist tyranny, relating to the individual and our fundamental human needs and desires. The accommodating or unifying moral concept is universal equality, which can be derived analytically, and has been derived historically, from each of these sources of authority and aspects of human nature (Rutherford, 1992).

Universal equality achieves some moderation when the concept of the dignity and worth of the individual is understood as a matter which requires the consideration and balancing of at least four different capacities and perspectives. Consider, for example, that the United States government was founded for the declared purposes of providing for the general welfare (legislated needs), establishing justice (adjudicated social conscience), maintaining domestic tranquility (executive order) and securing freedom for ourselves and our posterity (non-coercive meaning and purpose). In attempting to achieve institutional accommodation of these objectives on the basis of equality, this system of government does leave the question of meaning and purpose to the individual. This is what Jefferson, following Aristotle, meant by "the pursuit of happiness," which is quite different from the pursuit of pleasure as we understand it. The level of function that interprets, integrates, and narrates meaning, purpose, and continuity in our lives, and deals with the ultimate questions of metaphysics and religion, is separated from the coercive powers and structure of government. In turn, the individual moral personality is the basis of both our constitutional principles and democratic processes.

Universal equality is both the fundamental *qualitative moral principle* of our constitutional system of government and the basis of the *quantitative democratic process* by which it was ordained and ratified and by which it functions. We thus need to refer to our government as at least a *constitutional democracy* in order to understand and convey its moral foundations.

Thomas Hobbes in *Leviathan* (1651/1981, pp. 82–6) wrote that all persons are equal in that they fear a violent death, and they are not only capable of killing one another, but also, in the state of nature, they are free to do so. It is not contradictory to state that constitutional democracy is also our way of ritualizing aggression and coercive power. We limit and divide the coercive powers of government and we vote. As Reinhold Niebuhr noted, "It is man's capacity for justice that makes democracy possible, but it is his tendency to injustice that makes it necessary" (1944, p. xi).

Abraham Lincoln, in his First Inaugural Address, stated that "a majority, held in restraint by constitutional checks and limitations, ... is the only true sovereign of a free people. Whoever rejects it, does, of necessity, fly to anarchy or to despotism." Representative democracy, the staggering of elective terms of office, the requirement of a super-majority to amend the Constitution, the Bill of Rights, and an independent judiciary with judicial review are some of the constitutional checks and limitations placed on transient majorities. Federalism is, in part, a recognition that equal does not mean identical.

Abortion

The organic framework of analysis is not meant to defend a particular conclusion, but it will help to understand the spectrum of moral and political considerations involved in a complex issue such as abortion. The example is also meant to show that what we perceive to be the facts in medicine are part of our considerations, though they are not the *sole* determinants of our values and decisions.

One original reason for abortion laws in Texas, the jurisdiction of *Roe vs. Wade,* was the very high mortality and morbidity of the procedure in a time before antibiotics. The current state of medical science also forms the criteria for the present laws relating to trimesters, which is in part related to the possible viability of the fetus. In addition, the technological aspects of genetic counseling, the treatment of infertility, and methods of birth control all affect the issue. These changing facts in *medical science* are one of the considerations in the decisions concerning abortion. There are also *social* issues for the physician. The physician is licensed by the state, for example, and has an obligation to abide by the laws of the society in which he or she practices. If the law permits abortions, then there is also a *metaphysical or religious* issue for patients, doctors and hospitals as to whether they want to choose or perform the procedure. Finally, there are the central issues of the *individual* rights and well being of both the mother and the fetus or unborn child. If one understands government to be a monopoly of coercive power, there are also the issues of privacy as opposed to what are the legitimate concerns of the state. On the other hand, there is also the political issue of the uses of taxation in a pluralistic society. If the morbidity and mortality of the procedure were the same as they were in 1900, however, the other issues concerning abortion would not be on the political agenda. Facts are important, and sometimes an overriding consideration, but they are not the *sole* determinants of our values.

VI. Further Observations and Conclusions

In the ecological organic framework of analysis, integration is concerned internally with a reconciliation of our mind's four capacities of interpretation, reason, social conscience, and appetite. External integration relates to a reconciliation of our metaphysical ideas, our relation to the natural world in which we live, our relation to society, and our own individual self-interest. This is perhaps better understood by examining the opposite concept of alienation. Discord and alienation often result when one of our levels of understanding is emphasized to the exclusion of the others, or when, as a society, we develop ideologies that relate to one of our concepts of metaphysics, nature, society, or human beings, but to the exclusion of the other three. In a pluralistic society there is a potential political problem when any one dimension of human nature is emphasized to the exclusion of the others or when any dimension of human nature is excluded or not taken into consideration.

Singular theories that have based order and moral authority on *only* material needs, an aspect of social conscience, reason, or a metaphysical or religious concept, or *only* on the individual, the state, natural science, or ideology have often led to disintegration and individual or communal tragedy. By focusing on even perhaps a particular truth in a quest for certainty, they have too easily justified the use of coercive force or been the cause of alienation. The quest for certainty understandably often seeks truth in only one parameter.

A general observation based on the ecological organic paradigm is that those philosophies that are founded on only one dimension of humanity or the world in which we live will come under pressure to modify and extend their constructs to accommodate the other dimensions, just as Ptolemy's model of the universe needed to continuously add epicycles to account for the observed data.

What some have described as our postmodern condition is the other side of the coin. It is a consequence of the fallacy of concluding that because a single parameter doesn't explain everything, it is invalid and thus cannot be used as a compass or a way of knowing anything. Some aspects of Western civilization have thus dispensed and discarded in chronological order religion (the Church, the Bible), nature, society, and interconnected individualism as a legitimate basis of knowledge or moral and political authority. This leaves one only with the certainty of a closed system of one's own subjective meaning, which in the language of philosophy is non-verifiable and in moral and political terms is unaccountable. As a Woody

Allen character in the movie *Bullets over Broadway* states, "The artist creates his own moral universe." A radical skepticism, which separates the knower from that which is known, can understandably lead to this type of alienation. It is popular in our times, however, because it can also be a rationalization for self-indulgence and liberty pushed to license. This version of postmodernism can mean simply never having to say you are sorry. A similar version of postmodernism, by denying an epistemological basis for anything, allows the validation of everything and can be summarized as having the philosophical insight that "stuff happens." Another possible criticism of much of current philosophy is that, like Bacon's criticism of scholasticism, it has become focused on the abstractions of language at the expense of relating to the world in which we live.

The ecological organic paradigm suggests an alternative between the extremes of modernism and postmodernism based on prudence and moderation rather than a quest for certainty or a radical skepticism. Recognizing even the very broad capacities of human nature provides a basis for the values needed to develop those potentials. Aristotle defined man as a political animal and such an assertion, for example, is a basis for values which are felt to be necessary and desirable for living in a community. We have done something similar with human rights in an attempt to define a threshold of values that the individual does not delegate to society or government. Concerns for such things as a level of universal education and stewardship of the environment are values based on our capacity for reason and practical wisdom related to nature. Freedom of opinion and a separation of church and state were accommodations which recognized the need to at least establish the conditions for spiritual and metaphysical values in a pluralistic society where devastating wars had been fought over such matters. Where Kant in his own mind separated theology from empirical knowledge, Jefferson was instrumental in only separating religion from the coercive powers of government. He understood that one of his most significant works

119

was the *Statute of Virginia for Religious Freedom*. This is a recognition that some of our highest aspirations, strongest commitments, and deepest faiths cannot and should not be coerced.

In the perspective of the ecological organic framework, social abilities, reason, and a coherent self with meaning and purpose are not just the slaves of the passions, but are themselves ends as well as means. Because there is variety in humanity and our development, because we have limited knowledge and are prone to error, because ecology changes, and because there will sometimes be conflicting motivations, desires, and goals, the values derived from such an understanding of humanity will at best be based on prudence, practical wisdom, and our own commitments rather than certainty.[14] On the other hand, what is also implied by the ecological organic paradigm is that if such capacities developed in natural and cultural evolution as adaptive coping mechanisms, then we probably ignore their balanced development and the values associated with such development at the expense of our own well-being and possibly in a pluralistic world at our own peril. The organic framework is not only compatible with a new Darwinian behavioral ecology, but also with folk psychology, which is based on introspection and a history of accumulated experience.

A consideration of a threshold of values based on the ecological organic paradigm should lead to a *reconsideration of pragmatism as a "balance of consciousness."* Such an understanding of practical action and thought or pragmatism, it could be argued, was not first put forward by Charles Pierce, William James and John Dewey, but by the Founding Documents of American constitutional democracy. An understanding of pragmatism as a "balance of consciousness," however, is probably no longer retrievable from subsequent interpretations, revisions and distortions.[15] For this reason, an ecological organic paradigm perhaps better accommodates the "balance of consciousness" of folk psychology as well as the dimensional moral philosophy of "depth" and "breadth" that has been described.

Like our genetic code, our cultural ideas have a lot of recessive, extraneous, duplicated and redundant material. There is a lot of stuff in the attic, basement, and garage that we pull out when it is needed. One of the more perceptive writers and statesman of our times, Vaclav Havel, has said that we need a declaration of interdependence; that we need to recognize that we are a part of the universe rather than the masters of it; and that we "are mysteriously connected to the universe.... just as the entire evolution of the universe is mirrored in us" (1994). Havel, the current President of the Czech Republic, also recently told law students at Stanford University that "If democracy is not only to survive but to expand successfully and resolve those conflicts of cultures, then, in my opinion, it must rediscover and renew its own transcendental origins. Human dignity, freedom and responsibility. . . . The source of these basic human potentials lies . . . . in man's relationship to that which transcends him. I think the fathers of American democracy knew this very well" (1995).

A contemporary version of the organic paradigm that is compatible with an affirmation of life and recognizes the dynamic aspects of our common humanity is a framework of analysis that can perhaps help us understand both of these statements of Havel concerning nature and transcendence. They will not necessarily be considered a dichotomy. Such a framework was understood by the Founding Fathers and it should be reconsidered. In Federalist No. 51, James Madison (1788/1987, p. 319) wrote, "But what is government itself but the greatest of all reflections on human nature?"

Notes

1. "The New Darwinian Naturalism in Political Theory" by Larry Arnhart (1995) is a pivotal article in evolutionary theory with extensive references. See also *The Origins of Virtue; Human Instincts and the Evolution of Cooperation* by Matt Ridley (1996), *Being There: Putting Brain, Body, and World Together Again* by Andy Clark (1997), *The Symbolic Species: The Co-evolution of Language and the Brain* by Terrence W. Deacon (1997),

and "Holistic Darwinism: 'Synergistic Selection' and the Evolutionary Process" by P. A. Corning (1997).

2. In the preface of *Evolving the Mind: On the Nature of Matter and the Origin of Consciousness* (1996, viii), A. G. Cairns-Smith wrote, "William James gave us a general resolution of this dilemma more than a hundred years ago. In a nutshell: *matter* is not what it seems. Or as we should say now there must be more to biological material than is summarized in the models of molecular biology. To make any sense of this we will come to dig a little deeper: science is not what it seems . . ."

3. "The Puzzle of Conscious Experience." by David J. Chambers (*Scientific American,* December 1995, 80–86) is a review of the various ideas about consciousness by neuroscientists.

4. See "Epistemology from an Evolutionary Point of View" by Michael Braidie (1994) in *Conceptual Issues in Evolution,* ed. Elliot Sober, for some of the current ideas in this field. Traditional evolutionary epistemology by itself, however, does not address well some of the existential problems of moral and political philosophy. Traditional evolutionary theory by itself does not address well the questions "What is the best way to live?" or "What about us somatic cells?"

5. Michael S. Gazzaniga in *Nature's Mind: The Biological Roots of Thinking, Emotions, Sexuality, Language and Intelligence* (1992, chap. 6) uses the designation "interpreter" to describe a special capacity residing in the left hemisphere of the brain which he believes to be the core of human belief formation. I use the term interpretation more as a functional capacity for integration and narrative, recognizing the significant importance of language, memory (Dykstra, 1987), and imagination or "vision" in this.

6. Perhaps the most interesting example of this opinion is in the first two paragraphs of *Pragmatism: A New Name for Some Old Ways of Thinking* by William James (1907/1990) in which he quotes Chesterton, "There are some people—and I am one of them—who think that the most practical and important thing about a man is still his view of the universe. . . . we think the question is not whether the theory of the cosmos

affects matters, but whether, in the long run, anything else effects them." James then writes, "I think with Mr. Chesterton in this matter."

7. Jordan Peterson, a psychologist, in *Maps of Meaning: The Architecture of Belief* (1999) notes that human beings are territorial and "that because people are capable of abstraction, the territories we defend can become abstract" (Lambert, 1998).

8. There is at least a third major early Western historical moral tradition that is Anglo-Saxon. This tradition was important for the development of individual rights and resistance to tyranny as well as consent and contract, but since the two World Wars this has been largely ignored in academic circles.

9. The distinction between morality and ethics would be only one of convention and compromise. The word "morality" is of Latin origin and the word "ethics" is of Greek origin and they both originally had the meaning of "custom(s)." In our time, however, a discussion of ethics often considers all possible positions, including the merely subjective. Some consider ethics to be only cultural and others want it to only refer to universals. Richard Rorty, one of the more widely known contemporary philosophers, believes that a primary aim of liberalism should be to avoid being cruel. Yet concerning epistemology he wrote, "I do not think there are any plain moral facts out there in the world, nor any truths independent of language, nor any neutral ground on which to stand and argue that either torture or kindness are preferable to the other" (1989, p. 173). Richard A. Posner, a judge of the U.S. Court of Appeals for the Seventh Circuit, began his Holmes Lecture at Harvard Law School in 1997 on "The Problematics of Moral and Legal Theory" with the assertion that all morality is local (1998, vol. 111, p. 1637). These can be compared to the position of Hadley Arkes, a professor of jurisprudence and political science at Amherst College. In *First Things: An Inquiry into the First Principles of Morals and Justice* he claims that there are universal first principles the denial of which would be a self-contradiction (1986, p. 426).

10. For Jefferson on universal equality see Padover (1943,

1032–34), Peterson (1977, p. 424), Jefferson (1785/1972, p. 142 and 227), and Boorstin (1987, p. 111–23).

11. Marvin Meyers, in his book on James Madison, *The Mind of the Founder,* concluded that, "in Madison's view of man," equality was the fundamental term (1981, xxii).

12. Alexis de Tocqueville, in *Democracy in America,* "advanced the influential thesis that equality is the fundamental theme and characteristic of American civilization" (Davis, 1990, p. 11). David Brion Davis, a prominent historian of the institution of slavery, has even concluded that the real antithesis of slavery is not freedom but equality (1990, p. 29).

13. In 1856, before his presidency, Abraham Lincoln stated, "Our government rests in public opinion. Whoever can change public opinion, can change the government, practically just so much. Public opinion, or [on?] any subject, always has a "central idea," from which all its minor thoughts radiate. That "central idea" in our political public opinion, at the beginning was, and until recently has continued to be, "the equality of men" (Basler 1953, vol. II, p. 385; see also Jaffa 1982, chap. XIV).

14. We will always have to take practical action without complete knowledge or certainty. Churchland (1995) in his description of neurophysiology explains how, through such mechanisms as parallel processing, pattern completion, and vector analysis, we are physiologically developed to be able to function without complete sensory information. Anyone within the field of science also understands that "facts" are contingent and always open to new evidence and interpretation.

15. Sidney Hook recognized the probable irreversible distortions of pragmatism even in 1974 when he wrote *Pragmatism and the Tragic Sense of Life* (1974, chap. 1).

References

Adams, Raymond D. and Maurice Victor. 1993. *Principles of Neurology,* Fifth Edition. New York; McGraw-Hill.

Allen, W. B. 1988. *George Washington: A Collection.* Indianapolis, IN: Liberty Fund, Inc..

American Medical Association. 1993. *Guides to the Evaluation of Permanent Impairment,* Fourth Edition. Chicago: American Medical Association.

Arkes, Hadley. 1986. *First Things: An Inquiry into the First Principles of Morals and Justice.* Princeton: Princeton University Press.

Arnhart, Larry. 1988. "Aristotle's Biopolitics: A Defense of Biological Teleology against Biological Nihilism." *Politics and the Life Sciences* 6:173–229.

Arnhart, Larry. 1995. "The New Darwinian Naturalism in Political Theory." *American Political Science Review* 89:389–98.

Axelrod, Robert. 1984. *The Evolution of Cooperation.* New York: HarperCollins.

Barrett, William. 1986. *Death of the Soul.* Garden City, N. Y.: Anchor Press/Doubleday.

Basler, Roy P., ed., 1953. *The Collected Works of Abraham Lincoln,* 8 vols. New Brunswick, N. J.: Rutgers University.

Boorstin, Daniel. 1989. "The Equality of the Human Species." In *Hidden History.* New York: Vintage Books, Random House.

Bradie, Michael. 1994. "Epistemology from an Evolutionary View." In *Conceptual issues in Evolutionary Biology,* ed. Elliot Sober. Cambridge, Mass.: MIT Press.

Breyer, Stephen. 1998. "Judicial Review: A Practicing Judge's Perspective." H. L. A. Hart Memorial Lecture, May 7, 1998, University College, Oxford.

Cairns-Smith, A. G. 1996. *Evolving the Mind: On the Nature of Matter and the Origin of Consciousness.* Cambridge: Cambridge University Press.

Cardozo, Benjamin. 1921. *The Nature of the Judicial Process.* New Haven: Yale University Press.

Chambers, David J. 1995. "The Puzzle of Conscious Experience." *Scientific American.* December 1995, 80–86.

Churchland, Paul M. 1995. *The Engine of Reason, the Seat of the Soul.* Cambridge, Mass.: MIT Press.

Clark, Andy. 1997. *Being There: Putting Brain, Body, and World Together Again.* Cambridge, Mass.: MIT Press.

Cornford, F. M. 1932. *Before and After Socrates.* Cambridge: Cambridge University Press.

Corning, P. A. 1997. "Holistic Darwinism: 'Synergistic Selection' and the Evolutionary Process." *Journal of Social and Evolutionary Systems,* 20:363-400.

Corwin, Edward S. 1955. *The "Higher Law" Background of American Constitutional Law.* Ithaca N. Y.: Cornell University.

Covey, Stephen R. 1989. *The 7 Habits of Highly Effective People.* Simon and Schuster: New York.

Darwin, Charles. 1936. *The Origin of Species and the Descent of Man.* New York: Random House.

Davis, David Brion. 1990. *Revolutions: Reflections on American Equality and Foreign Liberations.* Cambridge, Mass.: Harvard University.

Deacon, Terrence W. 1997. *The Symbolic Species: the Co-evolution of Language and the Brain.* New York: Norton.

DesAutels, Peggy. 1997. "Gestalt Shifts in Moral Reception." *In Mind and Morals: Essays on Cognitive Science and Ethics,* eds. Larry May, Marilyn Friedman, and Andy Clark. Cambridge, Mass.: MIT Press.

Dykstra, Craig. 1987. "Memory and Truth." *Theology Today,* vol. XLIV, No. 2.

Eccles, Sir John. 1989. *Evolution of the Brain: Creation of the Mind.* New York: Routledge.

Finley, John H., Jr. 1966. *The Four Stages of Greek Thought.* Stanford, California: Stanford University Press.

Flanagan, Owen. 1991. *The Science of the Mind,* Second Edition. Cambridge, Mass.: The MIT Press.

Flanagan, Owen. 1997. "Ethics Naturalized: Ethics in Human Ecology." *In Mind and Morals: Essays on Cognitive Science and*

Ethics, eds. Larry May, Marilyn Friedman, and Andy Clark. Cambridge Mass.: MIT Press.

Gazzaniga, Michael S. 1992. *Nature's Mind: The Biological Roots of Thinking, Emotions, Sexuality, Language and Intelligence.* New York: Basic Books.

Gilligan, Carol. 1982. *In A Different Voice,* Cambridge, Mass.: Harvard University Press.

Godfrey-Smith, Peter. 1996. *Complexity and the Function of the Mind in Nature.* Cambridge: Cambridge University Press.

Hale, David. 1973. "Analogy of the Body Politic." *In Dictionary of The History of Ideas,* ed. Philip P. Wiener. New York: Charles Scribner's Sons.

Havel, Vaclav. 1994. *Newsweek,* July 18, 1994, p.66.

Havel, Vaclav. 1995. "The Spiritual Roots of Democracy." Lapis (Summer), 27–30.

Henderson, Lawrence. 1970. *The Fitness of the Environment.* Boston: Beacon Hill.

Hook, Sidney. 1974. *Pragmatism and the Tragic Sense of Life.* New York: Basic Books.

Jaffa, Henry V. 1982 ed. *Crisis of the House Divided: An Interpretation of the Issues of the Lincoln-Douglas Debates.* Chicago: University of Chicago.

James, William. (1907/1990). *Pragmatism: A New Name for Some Old Ways of Thinking.* In *Great Books of the Western World,* vol. 55: 1–77, ed., Adler, Mortimer. Chicago: Encyclopedia Brittanica.

Jefferson, Thomas. (1785/1972). *Notes on the State of Virginia.* New York; W. W. Norton.

Kekes, John. 1989. *Moral Tradition and Individuality.* Princeton: Princeton University Press.

Kohlberg, Lawrence. 1981. *The Philosophy of Moral Development,* vol. I. San Francisco: Harper and Row.

Konner, Melvin. 1983. *The Tangled Wing: Biological Constraints on the Human Spirit.* New York: Harper Colophon.

Lachterman, David Rapport. 1989. *The Ethics of Geometry: A Genealogy of Modernity.* London: Routledge.

Lambert, Craig 1998. "Chaos, Culture, Curiosity." *Harvard Magazine,* vol. 101, no. 1: 20.

Lapsley, Daniel. 1992. "Pluralism, Virtues, and the Post-Kohlbergian Era in Moral Psychology." In *The Challenge of Pluralism: Education, Politics, and Values,* eds. F. Clark Power and Daniel K. Lapsley. Notre Dame: University of Notre Dame Press.

Lennox, James G. 1993. "Darwin was a Teleologist." *Biology and Philosophy,* 8:409–21.

Letwin, Shirley. 1982. *The Gentleman in Trollope; Individuality and Moral Conduct.* Cambridge, MA: Harvard University Press.

Lewis, C.S. 1943. *Mere Christianity.* New York: Macmillan.

Lippman, Walter. 1955. *The Public Philosophy.* New York: New American Library.

Madison, James, Hamilton, A. and Jay, J. (1788/1987). *The Federalist Papers.* London: Penguin.

Mayr, Ernst. 1988. *Toward a New Philosophy of Biology: Observations of an Evolutionist.* Cambridge, Mass.: Harvard University Press.

Minogue, Kenneth. 1983. "The Culture of the Gentleman." *Public Interest,* No. 71, Spring.

Meyers, Marvin, ed., 1981. *The Mind of the Founder: Sources of the Political Thought of James Madison,* revised ed. Hanover, N.H.: Brandeis University.

Mithen, Steven. 1996. *The Prehistory of the Mind.* New York: Thames and Hudson.

Nagel, Thomas. 1972. "Aristotle on Eudaimonia." *Phronesis,* 17:252–259.

Niebuhr, Reinhold. 1944. *The Children of Light and the Children of Darkness.* New York: Scribner's.

Orsini, G. N. G. 1973. "Organicism" In *The Dictionary of the History of Ideas,* ed. Phillip P. Wiener. New York: Charles Scribner's Sons.

Padover, Saul K. ed., 1943. *The Complete Jefferson.* New York: Tudor Publishing.

Penrose, Roger. 1994. *Shadows of the Mind: A Search for the*

Missing Science of Consciousness. Oxford: Oxford University Press.

Peterson, Jordan. 1988. *Maps of Meaning: The Architecture of Belief.* New York and London: Routledge.

Peterson, Merrill D. ed., 1977. *The Portable Thomas Jefferson.* New York: Penguin Books.

Posner, Richard A. 1998. "The Problematics of Moral and Legal Theory." *Harvard Law Review,* vol. 111, 1637.

Post, John F. 1996. "The Foundationalism in Irrealism, and the Immorality." *Journal of Philosophical Research,* vol. XXI: 1–14.

Quine, W. V. 1969. "Epistemology Naturalized." In *Ontological Relativity and other Essays.* W. V. Quine. 1996. New York: Columbia University Press.

Rawls, John. 1971. *A Theory of Justice.* Cambridge, Mass.: Harvard University Press.

Rawls, John. 1993. *Political Liberalism.* New York: Columbia University Press.

Ridley, Matt. 1996. *The Origins of Virtue: Human Instincts and the Evolution of Cooperation.* New York: Penguin Books.

Roberts, Clayton and David Roberts. 1980. *A History of England,* 2 vol. Englewood Cliffs, N. J.: Prentice- Hall.

Rorty, Richard. 1989. *Contingency, Irony, and Solidarity.* Cambridge: Cambridge University Press.

Rutherford, James. 1992. *The Moral Foundations of United States Constitutional Democracy.* Pittsburgh: Dorrance.

Sacks, Oliver. 1995. *An Anthropologist from Mars: Seven Paradoxical Tales.* New York: Knopf.

Sagan, Carl. 1977. *The Dragons of Eden: Speculations on the Evolutions of Human Intelligence.* New York: Ballantine Books.

Stevenson, Leslie. 1987. *Seven Theories of Human Nature.* New York: Oxford University.

Weber, Max. (1921/1964). *The Theory of Social and Economic Organization,* 1st paperback edition, ed., Talcott Parsons. New York: Free Press.

Wilson, James Q. 1993. *The Moral Sense.* New York: Free Press.

Wittgenstein, Ludwig. 1922. *Tractatus Logico–Philosophicus,* tr. by C. K. Ogden. London: Routledge.

An earlier version of the following essay was given as a paper at the World Congress of Philosophy 2003 in Istanbul, Turkey.

What Medical Ethics Have to Offer the Larger Fields of Moral and Political Philosophy

Abstract

The four principles of medical ethics—beneficence, nonmaleficence, justice, and autonomy—can be interpreted as being based on a respect for human life. Human life, however, is understood to be multidimensional. Like folk psychology, medical ethics understands there to be physical, social, mental, and metaphysical or spiritual aspects of human nature. The four principles of bioethics are also compatible with the concepts of equality derived from four different moral and legal systems in Western civilization which had their separate foundations in religion, nature, society, and the individual. Medical ethics are also based on both nature and culture. There is thus a relationship between the concept of a respect for human life in medical ethics and the concept of equality in the Western liberal political tradition. The multidimensional conception of human nature was largely discarded in moral and political philosophy, however, because it was originally hierarchical and used to justify the rule of the Pope and the king. One of the primary insights of modern medicine is that it uses these same categories to describe the multiple dimensions of human nature, but not necessarily in a hierarchical manner. These categories should thus be reconsidered as a very useful framework of analysis for the larger fields of moral and political philosophy.

Medical ethics are based on more than one parameter and therefore they do not necessarily lead to certainty. They also, however, do not lead to a situation where everything is subjective, relative, arbitrary, or based only on material needs because they are all based on a respect for an aspect of human life. They represent a balance of consciousness.

In this context, medical ethics have a lot to offer the larger fields of moral and political philosophy. Much of modern philosophy can be compared to the blind man describing the elephant; each perspective describes a particular part, but none gives a coherent view of the "elephant."

*Medical ethics bring some coherence to the moral cate-
gories. They are also one source of an applied moral philosophy that can enable cross-cultural understanding and ethical
dialogue. Medical ethics have at least the capacity to provide a
well-balanced source of affirmation, accommodation, moderation, coherence, and synthesis in a pluralistic global community.*

What Medical Ethics Have to Offer the Larger Fields of Moral and Political Philosophy

Introduction

Medical ethics have a lot to offer the larger fields of moral
and political philosophy at this particular time in history, in
part, because they have the capacity to accommodate pluralism in a global community. Medical ethics can be interpreted
as being based on three axioms or assertions along with a cou-
ple of relevant observations.

1. The *primary moral assertion or premise of medical ethics
   is a respect for human life.*
2. Modern medicine *understands human nature to be multidimensional.* The four general principles of bioethics or
   medical ethics are:
   Beneficence (the Golden Rule—do unto others as you
   would have them do unto you—reciprocity—benefit
   the patient)
   Nonmaleficence (the Silver Rule—don't do unto others
   what you don't want them to do unto you—reversibi-
   ity—do no harm)
   Justice (social justice)
   Autonomy (individual rights).[1]
   These four principles of bioethics can be interpreted as
   being based on a respect for the multidimensional
   aspects of human nature. The four principles also relate
   to different aspects of the moral concept of equality and
   they are derived primarily from, in turn, metaphysics,
   nature, society, and individual concerns. This perspective provides some coherence to the ethical categories.

132

3. Medical ethics understands the nature/nurture controversy about human nature to be a both/and rather than an either/or issue. Medical ethics are based on the life sciences as well as cultural factors.
4. Based on these initial moral assertions, medical ethics can be shown to be compatible with a moral system that has both "depth" (a capacity for a distinction of values) and "breadth" (a capacity for inclusion).
5. Medical ethics are based on the applied science of medicine and its initial axioms or principles can thus also be derived inductively as maxims from experience. Medical ethics can also provide a vehicle for cross-cultural dialogue and understanding. They have the capacity to accommodate pluralism in a global community.

Medical Ethics

1. A respect for human life

As a physician I consider a respect for human life to be the primary moral principle of the medical profession. The Declaration of Geneva of the World Medical Association includes this principle of a respect for human life.[2] This does not, however, mean preserving life at all costs.

A respect for human life is a moral assertion. Even the initial axioms or assertions of mathematics though, such as the definition of a line, are contingent and not proven. Our methods of description in physics also shift at the extremes of quantum mechanics and relativity and the two have not as yet been reconciled. The capacity to perceive a straight line, however, and even the illusion of a straight line, was important in evolution and remains important for our survival and well-being.[3] The same can be said for the foundations of medical ethics. If one postulates the goals of human prosperity and posterity, then moral and political values become conditional factors for achieving these ends.[4] It is for these reasons, a hypothetical imperative if you will, that in the coming century biology rather than physics will become the prevailing paradigm.

A respect for human life also implies a concept of equality

133

understood as an inherent dignity and worth of our common humanity. The concept of "all men are created equal" was for Thomas Jefferson an affirmation of his own individuality, but it was also his recognition of our common humanity, or, a categorical imperative. Abraham Lincoln described the phrase "all men are created equal" as the central idea of our government.[5,6] Jefferson believed that all human beings, including American Indians and blacks, have a moral sense.[7] Like a muscle, however, this human capacity needs to be developed through exercise. For Jefferson it was our universal moral capacity that makes self-government possible. The great reformers in American history did not repudiate the ideal of equality, but asked that we live up to it. The moral assertion of "a respect for human life" in medical ethics is also such a self-affirmation and a recognition of our common humanity. It is this fundamental principle or moral assertion, this affirmation of human dignity and worth, this categorical imperative which recognizes our common humanity, that makes the accommodation and preservation of a wide variety of attributes, cultural differences, desires, and beliefs possible in a pluralistic world.

A respect for human life can also be derived from historical and social sources, as well as from natural (the hypothetical imperative) and metaphysical (the categorical imperative) considerations as above. Thomas Beauchamp and James Childress developed and taught the four principles of bioethics in their successive editions of the book *Principles of Biomedical Ethics.* They consider the four principles to be derived from the common morality (or all those who are serious about moral conduct and their moral responsibilities) and the historical moral traditions of medicine. These are social and cultural sources. They specifically, however, state that "in this 'theory,' there is no single unifying principle or concept— a traditional goal of ethical theory that seems now to be fading fast."[8] It should be noted, however, that neither Beauchamp nor Childress is a physician. More importantly, the moral assertion of a respect for human life can accommodate and be the basis for each of their described principles when human life and the world in which we live are understood to be multidimensional. Intuitionism is the view that there is a plurality of moral principles, each of which we can know directly. Beauchamp and Childress relied extensively on the intuitionist account of *prima facie* values by W.D. Ross in *The Right and the Good* (1930)[9]. Robert Audi is Professor of Philosophy and Professor of Business Ethics at the University of Notre Dame and Editor in Chief of *The Cambridge Dictionary of Philosophy*. In a recent work, *The Good and the Right: A Theory of Intuition and Intrinsic Value* (2004), Professor Audi also relies extensively on the work of W. D. Ross and concludes that, "In the practical domain, as in theoretical ethics, respect for persons is the fundamental attitude appropriate to the dignity of persons, and the dignity of persons is the central higher-order pervasive value that encompasses the other values essential in grounding moral obligation."[10]

A respect for human life can also be derived from individual and human rights concerns. In moral theory we see this in the history of human rights. More recently this is seen in the capabilities approach of Amartya Sen, a Nobel Prize winning economist.[11] In medical ethics this is part of those theories that are based on induction from specific cases (casuistry) and those that begin with our common needs, aspirations and desires.

A respect for human life can thus be supported from the perspective of metaphysics, nature, society and the individual. A multidimensional understanding of human nature can be inclusive of our physical, social, mental, and psychic or spiritual needs. It is this multidimensional understanding of human nature and our interaction with the world in which we live that give some coherence to the several ethical categories. Deontological (duty based), consequential, communitarian, and individual (human rights) concepts are all included in this meta-ethical perspective. Virtue ethics and an ethics of care are similar umbrella concepts that would recognize the multiple aspects of human nature, but from a particular perspective.

2. The Multidimensional Aspects of Human Nature

A multidimensional framework for the understanding of human nature is not a modern or postmodern idea. It is a premodern idea. The classical Greeks understood human nature to be a composite whole and to have physical, social, mental, and spiritual dimensions. They also perceived these different aspects of human nature to have a correlation to various aspects of the world in which we live. These ideas were often referred to as an organic paradigm. This multidimensional understanding of human nature, however, was eventually discarded and replaced in Western philosophy primarily because it was hierarchical in its Platonic form, as the tripartite soul, and it had been used to support similar hierarchical structures in the Church and the state.

A primary insight of modern medicine is that it uses the same categories as the classical organic paradigm for understanding human nature, but it does not necessarily interpret the several dimensions of human nature to be hierarchical. This allows us to reconsider a modern version of the organic paradigm as a framework of analysis in a modern context.[12]

The organic paradigm was replaced in Western philosophy primarily by utilitarianism, which attempts to calculate the greatest good for the greatest number based on pleasure and pain. Consider, however, a current multidimensional model used in medicine to evaluate pain.[13]

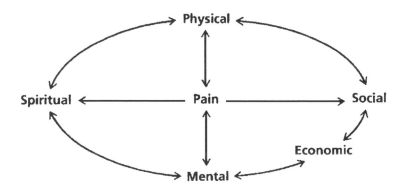

136

Even utilitarian calculations of the greatest good, based on pleasure and pain, are thus seen to depend on the same categories as the older organic paradigm and the framework is not necessarily hierarchical.

The classical organic paradigm was also replaced in Western political theory primarily by the concept of social contract. The categories of the organic paradigm, however, are also important for an analytical and historical understanding of equality, which is the basis of social contract theory as well as the underlying presumption of utilitarianism. In *The Moral Foundations of United States Constitutional Democracy: an Analytical and Historical Inquiry into the Primary Moral Concept of Equality* (1992), James Rutherford (the author of this essay on medical ethics), previously described the multiple origins of the concept of equality in Western civilization.[14] These included a *metaphysical origin* in Judeo-Christian religion based on reverence and reciprocity, which was expressed in Canon law; *a natural law origin* in Roman law based on reason and reversibility; a *communitarian origin* in English common law based on one's rights and responsibilities in society; and finally an *individual origin* in social contract theory, which is the basis of constitutional law and which begins with the free and equal individual in a state of nature concerned with human rights and the right to resist tyranny.

American constitutional democracy integrates and balances these four ethical systems as they relate to universal equality and the coercive powers of government. The Declaration of Independence was written in the manner of Euclidean geometry. The first moral assertion of the Declaration of Independence that "all men are created equal" thus placed everything that followed, including life, liberty, and the pursuit of happiness, in this moral context. The Preamble of the Constitution describes the purposes of government to be to provide for the general welfare, to establish justice, and to maintain security and domestic tranquility or rational order. These are provided primarily by a division and balancing of the powers of government by function rather than social class

137

with a legislature, a judiciary, and an executive branch. The metaphysics of religion and public opinion are also recognized and they are protected and separated from the coercive powers of government.

The four principles of biomedical ethics, as described by Beauchamp and Childress, are considered to be *prima facie* principles, meaning that they each hold unless they need to be modified because they are in conflict with another moral obligation or one of the other principles. The concept of a respect for human life in medical ethics and the concept of equality in American constitutional democracy are both based on a respect for persons, an affirmation of our individual dignity and worth, and our common humanity. They are also both based on a multidimensional understanding of human nature and this is reflected in both as a system of checks and balances.

This four-part multidimensional framework can accommodate both natural and cultural evolution. It can accommodate both prescriptive and descriptive concepts of human nature and it can accommodate both the individual and social dimensions of human knowledge and activity. The framework gives some coherence to the ethical categories. The questions, *What is obligatory?*, *What is good?*, *What is fitting?*, and *What is humane?* are all included within the framework as valid moral questions. Deontological, consequential, communitarian and individual human concerns are all recognized within a historical perspective as well. Medical ethics represent a balance of consciousness in what some have described as the parliament of the mind.

This four-part analytical framework can be contrasted with the general state of philosophy in the last one hundred years, which might be compared to the story of the blind men describing the elephant; each perspective describes a particular part, but none gives a coherent view of the elephant. This four-part framework of analysis brings some coherence to the ethical categories.

3. The nature/nurture controversy about human nature is a both/and situation

From the time of Hippocrates, the profession of medicine has been based on both science and an ethic. Medicine thus easily incorporates an understanding of human nature that includes both nature and nurture. Medicine is not just descriptive, but it is also prescriptive. In medicine our perception of the facts is important and sometimes an overriding consideration, but facts are not the *sole* determinants of our values. In moral philosophy and medicine we do not accept a description of "what is" to be necessarily right. A reality principle and the sciences, however, also place constraints on our individual and social will. Darwinian evolution and nature on the one hand and cultural evolution on the other hand are both important because they place limitations on each other. As a result of sexual reproduction, the human body is made up of both genetic cells and somatic cells. The genetic cells at least have the possibility of reproduction, and continuity—the somatic cells in natural circumstances do not. What about us somatic cells? The somatic cells are concerned also about the quality of life. Moral philosophy is thus concerned about both posterity and prosperity, about Darwinian survival and reproduction and also our individual and cultural well-being. Darwinian concepts of evolution need to incorporate some concepts of our capacity for cultural evolution and cultural historicism needs to extend history back into evolutionary time.[15,16,17]

4. A moral system of "depth" and "breadth"

Much of our discourse could be clarified by recognizing both "breadth" and "depth" in moral philosophy. There are, for example, two great moral traditions in Western civilization. The first is from classical civilization and is based primarily on a distinction of values regarding such things as truth, goodness and beauty and such qualities as virtue. The second concerns the equal dignity and worth of individuals as persons and is derived primarily from Judeo-Christian sources, such as the Golden Rule and imago Dei and later Kant's categorical imperative. The concept of moral "depth," refers to an affirmation of life and a *distinction of values that relates primarily to attributes and behavior.* The concepts of moral "breadth" extends this affirmation to the individual, the social community, our common humanity, concerns about the natural world in which we live, and metaphysical concepts of meaning and purpose. For a moral system to have sufficient "breadth," for example, there needs to be a *respect for persons and an affirmation of our common humanity.* The two ethical systems are often confused in *dialogue* when there is no recognition of the difference between an *equality of persons* and *a distinction of values that relates to attributes and behavior.* There can be "moral" positions that are "narrow" and "shallow."

5. Medical ethics as an applied ethics

Medicine is an applied science and the principles of medical ethics have thus also been derived inductively as maxims from experience and case studies. Folk psychology, which relates to every day experiences, also intuitively recognizes the physical, social, mental, and spiritual aspects of human nature. These categories are compatible with those described in the organic paradigm and medical ethics. The medical profession has essentially universal recognition and medicine is a social institution that has the capacity to "expand the circle of trust," build social capital, and help maintain morality and order without coercion or alienation. Medical ethics are one source of applied moral philosophy that can provide cross-cultural understanding and enable ethical dialogue. Medical ethics have the capacity to provide a well-balanced source of affirmation, accommodation, moderation, coherence, and synthesis in a pluralistic global community.

An Example of Using the Framework of Analysis

The organic framework of analysis is not meant to defend a particular conclusion, but it will help to understand the spectrum of moral and political considerations involved in a complex difficult issue such as abortion in a pluralistic society. The example is also meant to show that what we perceive to be the facts in medicine are part of our considerations, though they are not the *sole* determinants of our values and decisions.

One original reason for abortion laws in Texas, the jurisdiction of *Roe vs. Wade,* was the very high mortality and morbidity of the procedure in a time before antibiotics. The current state of medical science also forms the criteria for the present laws relating to trimesters, which are in part related to the possible viability of the fetus. In addition, the technological aspects of genetic counseling, the treatment of infertility, and methods of birth control all affect the issue. These changing facts in *medical science* are one of the considerations in the decisions concerning abortion. There are also *social* issues for the physician. The physician is licensed by the state, for example, and has an obligation to abide by the laws of the society in which he or she practices. If the law permits abortions, then there is also a *metaphysical or religious* issue for patients, doctors, and hospitals as to whether they want to choose or perform the procedure. Finally, there are the central issues of the *individual* rights and well-being of both the mother and the fetus or unborn child. If one understands government to be a monopoly of coercive power, there are also the issues of privacy as opposed to what are the legitimate concerns of the state. On the other hand, there is also the political issue of the uses of taxation in a pluralistic society. If the morbidity and mortality of the procedure were the same as they were in 1900, however, the other issues concerning abortion would not be on the political agenda. Our perception of the facts are important, and sometimes an overriding consideration, but they are not the *sole* determinates of our values.

Most of the issues in medicine are not this complex, but when there are significant conflicts one frequently falls back on a procedure which one thinks is an appropriate means that also does justice to the ends. This is the case with voting in a democracy and the function of the jury and the Supreme Court in the legal field. The practice of medicine is primarily a voluntary relationship. Once the legal mandates are clear, the decisions usually rest on and require the informed consent of the individual patient. Medical science issues and metaphysical issues, however, can also play a significant role.

Summary and Conclusions

Contrary to the prevailing view of principlism in medical ethics, the moral assertion is made in this essay that a respect for human life is the foundation of the four principles of beneficence, non-maleficence, justice and autonomy. The four principles in medical ethics also relate to the several historical concepts of equality in United States constitutional democracy, as both are based on the dignity and worth of persons, and an affirmation of both our individuality and our common humanity.

In this framework, human nature is understood to be multidimensional with individual, social, rational/scientific, and integrative/metaphysical concerns. It is this "balance of consciousness" that brings some coherence to the meta-ethical categories in moral philosophy. A consideration of what is right, good, fitting, and humane can all be included.

This framework of analysis, which has been described as a modern ecological organic paradigm, is particularly effective in evaluating singular theories in philosophy which focus on only one aspect of human nature or those philosophies which exclude a particular aspect of human nature. One often does not have to argue that those philosophies are wrong, but only that they are not inclusive enough.

An affirmation of human dignity and worth can be derived from individual, social, natural and metaphysical sources. On the other hand, this affirmation, which is a moral assertion, also has implications for practical action that relate to basic individual needs and desires, social concerns, natural material consequences, and metaphysical perspectives. It can be both descriptive and prescriptive. A multidimensional understanding of human nature does not necessarily lead to certainty, but it also does not consider everything to be sub-

142

jective, relative, arbitrary, or based only on material utility. This framework of analysis thus addresses what some consider to be the postmodern dilemma. This four-part analytical framework, of which medical ethics is an example, may eventually become identified with both a new interpretation of pragmatism as a "balance of consciousness" and a "naturalized" epistemology, which also recognizes integrative/metaphysical, adaptive considerations and perspectives.

Biology, rather than physics, will probably become the prevailing paradigm of this century. This will not happen, however, until it adopts a similar type of methodology concerning human nature which is based in the life sciences, but is also broad enough to include the natural sciences, the social sciences, and the humanities.

The principles and moral assertions of medical ethics put forth here are a respect for human life, that there are multiple dimensions of human nature, and that nature and nurture are both important for they place some limitations on each other concerning our values. Medical ethics are an example of a very useful four-part framework of analysis for moral and political philosophy that also provides some coherence to the moral categories. They are one source of an applied moral philosophy that can provide cross-cultural understanding and enable ethical dialogue. In a political context, medical ethics can provide a well-balanced source of affirmation, accommodation, moderation, coherence, and synthesis in a pluralistic world. Medical ethics have a lot to offer the larger fields of moral and political philosophy at this particular time in history, in part, because they have the capacity to accommodate pluralism in a global community.

References

1. Tom L. Beauchamp and James F. Childress, *Principles of Biomedical Ethics,* Fifth Edition *(New York: Oxford University Press, 2000).*
2. Albert R. Jonsen, Mark Siegler, and William J. Winslade, *Clinical Ethics: A Practical Approach to Ethical Decisions in Clinical Medicine, Fourth Edition* (New York: McGraw-Hill, 1998), p.145.
3. Andrew Parker, *In the Blink of an Eye,* (Cambridge, MA: Perseus Publishing, 2003).
4. Peter A. Corning, "Biological Adaptation in Human Societies: a 'Basic Needs' Approach", *Journal of Bioeconomics* 2: 41–86, 2000.
5. Roy P. Basler, ed., 1953. *The Collected Works of Abraham Lincoln,* 8 vols. (New Brunswick, N.J.: Rutgers University), vol. II, p 385.
6. Henry V. Jaffa, 1982 ed., *Crisis of the House Divided: An Interpretation of the Issues in the Lincoln-Douglas Debates,* (Chicago: University of Chicago), chap. XIV.
7. Thomas Jefferson, *Notes on the State of Virginia* (New York: Routledge, 1785/1972), p.142.
8. Tom L. Beauchamp and James F. Childress, *Principles of Biomedical Ethics, Fifth Edition* (New York: Oxford University Press, 2000), p.405.
9. W. D. Ross, *The Right and the Good* (Oxford: Oxford University Press, 1930).
10. Robert Audi, *The Good in the Right: A Theory of Intuition and Intrinsic Value* (Princeton: Princeton University Press, 2004), p. 201.
11. Amartya Sen, *Development as Freedom,* (New York: Anchor Books, 2000), p. 77.
12. James H. Rutherford, "An Ecological Organic Paradigm: A Framework of Analysis for Moral and Political Philosophy," *Journal of Consciousness Studies,* 1999, 6 (10): 81–103. *http://www.organicparadigm.com*

13. American Medical Association, *Guide to the Evaluation of Permanent Impairment, Fourth Edition* (Chicago: American Medical Association, 1993), p. 307.
14. James H. Rutherford, *The Moral Foundations of United States Constitutional Democracy: An Analytical and Historical Inquiry into the Primary Moral Concept of Equality* (Pittsburgh, Pa.: Dorrance Publishing, 1992) *http://www. moralfoundations.com*
15. Hilary Putnam, *The Collapse of the Fact/Value Dichotomy and Other Essays* (Cambridge, MA: Harvard University Press, 2002).
16. Steven Pinker, *The Blank Slate: The Modern Denial of Human Nature* (New York: Viking Penguin, 2002).
17. Matt Ridley, *Nature via Nurture,* (New York: HarperCollins Publishers, 2003).

Distinguished Alumni Award
Westlake High School, 1994

On an Occasion to Honor my Father,
Judge Leland Rutherford

Winston Churchill said that courage is the greatest of the virtues because it is what makes all of the other virtues possible. This was not a new thought. Aristotle also considered courage to be the primary virtue. What I have learned from my father, however, is that it is love that makes courage possible.

Woody Hayes, the Ohio State football coach, borrowed from the writings of Ralph Waldo Emerson when he used to say that we don't so much pay back in our lives as we pay forward. I have always, in this manner, attributed the love of my father for his family and his character to be a tribute to his parents, and especially his father whom I never knew. My father has paid forward.

In addition to a love of his family, my father had a love for his work as a judge for forty-two years. I always perceived his love of justice and the law to be a moral passion. I understood it to be based on at least an ideal similar to what Atticus Finch described in a closing argument in *To Kill a Mockingbird:*

> But there is one way in this country in which all men are created equal—there is one human institution that makes a pauper the equal of a Rockefeller, the stupid man the equal of an Einstein, and the ignorant man the equal of any college president. That institution, gentlemen, is a court. It can be the Supreme Court of the United States or the humblest J. P. court in the land, or this honorable court which you serve. Our courts have their faults, as does any human institution, but in this country our courts are the great levelers, and in our courts all men are created equal.

My father would probably not see himself as a courageous man. He would perhaps see himself as a religious man. I have observed my father in times of both disappointment and success, however, and what I have learned is that it is love that makes courage possible.